THROUGH OTHER EYES

Through Other Eyes

Vivid Narratives of ❤ Some of the Bible's
Most Notable Characters

Carl E. Price

THE UPPER ROOM
Nashville, Tennessee

The scripture used in this book has been quoted or paraphrased from the Revised Standard Version of the Bible, copyrighted 1946, 1952, and © 1971 by the Division of Christian Education, National Council of Churches of Christ in the United States of America and is used by permission.

Book and Cover Design: Nancy G. Johnstone
First Printing: April 1987 (5)
Library of Congress Catalogue Card Number: 86-051153
ISBN: 0-8358-0555-7
Printed in the United States of America

To my

Mother,

Wanda Evelyn Johnson,

with

love.

CONTENTS

INTRODUCTION

The gospel was not originally given to us in a book or on parchment scrolls but in a person, and it was to persons that God was revealed and Christ made himself known. Those persons were men and women of a time and a place. Their culture, their personalities, and their experiences became a part of the medium through which the message came. So it is that we can often find deeper understandings of God's word in scripture for our time when we seek to enter into the life and times of those who lived long ago and heard and felt and saw what has been recorded as the actions and revelations of God.

One of the ways we can be helped in this understanding is through the work of archaeologists and historians, who help us discover what the land, the culture, and the environment of a particular period of history was like. It is of only passing interest to know that one can stand on the Mount of Olives and look southeast and see the sun reflecting on the Dead Sea and then look south and see two mountains, one of which is slightly higher than the other. It adds but little to learn that the taller mountain was the site of Herod's summer palace. Our interest may be heightened a bit when we learn that the two mountains were of equal height until Herod had his workmen remove the top of the one and place it on the crest of the other in order to increase its height and give him better visibility and a military advantage. But add to these facts of geography the reminder that it was on the Mount of Olives that Jesus spoke his word about faith moving a mountain into the sea, and this bit of scripture seems to come alive in a new way! To learn that the tables of Jesus' day were very low to the floor and that guests reclined around them on their side with their feet extended away from the table may take something away from Leonardo da Vinci's painting, but it adds a great deal to the understanding of how a woman could bathe Jesus' feet with her tears while he sat at table and of how John could speak of one of the disciples leaning on Jesus' breast. We owe no small debt to those who share such knowledge with us. Indeed, to miss such details is often to misinterpret the gospel.

Another way in which we are helped in understanding is through efforts to "get inside" of the people themselves, to try to see and feel through their eyes and emotions. This is no doubt less exact and verifiable than archaeology, but there is still a sense in which human personalities do not change all that much. The events and circumstances that impact human life may differ significantly and the particular fears and hopes may differ greatly, but feelings about fears and hopes and dreams remain remarkably similar through the years. This book is an effort to enter into some of those lives and thereby deepen our own awareness of that word that came in a particular time and place and seeks to make itself known in all times and places.

I make no claim that events described in this book had to happen with the particular details that I have added to some of the stories, but I hope the suggested details will strengthen the message rather than detract from it. Certainly, there is no intention to create some different message. While I have placed fictional details around people and events, I have tried to do so with a commitment to rather minimal elaboration, only enough to bring the characters in the account more into our own awareness as real individuals of flesh and blood, with feelings not unlike our own.

To suggest that we need to see the gospel "through other eyes" is not to suggest that we do not need to see it through our own. Indeed, the word for our time may be quite different than the word for an earlier time, yet the application for our day is usually better made through an understanding of the earlier event.

After publication of my earlier book of similar narratives, *Writings in the Dust,* I heard from several groups who were using the book in study settings. Therefore, I have provided a few discussion questions for each chapter of *Through Other Eyes* to encourage such use. This is the point at which the applications for our own time come into focus, and without that we are missing the intent of this book. These questions are by no means considered the only direction in which the discussion might go, and those using the book for individual reading might find the questions helpful for further meditation and thought even if there is no one present with whom to discuss them. Ministers may find the questions helpful in developing sermons on the scripture passage involved.

I am indebted to the members of the Forum Class of First United Methodist Church of Midland, Michigan, for their help in developing the discussion questions through the use of several of the chapters as a basis for Sunday morning classes. My thanks also to the secretaries and volunteers at First United Methodist Church for their help in typing and proofing the manuscript; to my wife Pat for her help with suggestions and editing; to the congregations who have heard many of these thoughts in sermon form and who have provided the opportunity and encouragement to develop them; and to Janice Grana and the staff of The Upper Room for their prodding, suggestions, and encouragement in the development of the manuscript.

Finally, a word of deep appreciation to Dr. James Fleming—scholar, teacher, and friend. My study sessions under his guidance at the Jerusalem Center for Biblical Studies have provided numerous insights and details that have helped me see and experience some of the gospel through other eyes.

If in some small way this book enables you to do the same, my efforts will have been rewarded in a most satisfying way.

THROUGH OTHER EYES

1.

REDIGGING OLD WELLS

Genesis 12:1-4, 26:12-25

Isaac looked at his servants busily packing his camp and felt depressed. The black goatskin tent was being dismantled and folded now. The inner furnishings and deep carpets were already rolled and bundled, ready to load onto camels that stood waiting nearby. The flocks of sheep and goats had left the day before because they moved so much more slowly. The camel herds would travel with the caravan itself. Some of Isaac's servants had gone ahead, and some would travel with him. It was a massive task to move so many people and possessions, and he hated to leave a place that had been his home for so long. But he guessed that moving was better than the open conflict that would come if he stayed.

It was unfair. He had worked hard for what he had accumulated here. True, his fields and flocks had multiplied beyond expectation. Year after year twin lambs and kids had dotted the hillsides of spring in larger numbers than reasonable, bouncing across the pastures like whitecaps on a tossing sea. Even many of the she-camels had had multiple births. The fields he sowed seemed to green earlier than those around him, and being first to have crops to sell resulted in better prices. His servants increased, and his possessions multiplied until he had become the envy of those around him. But envy, he soon learned, was a mixed honor. He relished the deference and respect shown him when he appeared in the villages, but then he began to notice a sort of veiled hostility. The smiles were not real; the greetings seemed perfunctory, as if they were something the people didn't really want to do but thought they had to. Envy had blossomed into resentment. After a while he began to realize that the people were actually afraid of him! He thought the idea ridiculous, but his opinion did not change their attitudes. There seemed to be something about size and prosperity that invited anger. He didn't know what to make of it or what to do about it, but the attitude was unmistakably clear to him. What he had he had come by honestly and mostly by hard work. To be sure, there was the unexpected fruitfulness of his flocks and fields, but that was not something that he had attained at the expense of his neighbors. Why should they resent it because he was more fortunate than they? Yes, he had traded shrewdly and wisely and usually to his own profit, but he had not cheated anyone. What was to be resented in that? His neighbors did as much whenever they could, and some were not above the thumb on the balance or false bottoms in the measuring jars. He had simply traded more and in greater volume. Wealth makes wealth. It always had and it always would.

Then, of course, there was the Promise. His father, Abraham, had been a faithful servant of the Most High. The promise made long ago in Haran that he would be blessed and would prosper had been fulfilled, giving Isaac a good beginning in life. It even appeared that the Promise would continue through his son. Now Isaac was not so sure.

What people fear and resent they often try to destroy. And in the process, justice can often be denied the wealthy as well as the poor, he thought. Now things had come to a head; but there was nothing he could do unless he was willing to go to war with these people. He had prospered so well that the people had complained to the king. Finally, Abimelech had ordered him to leave their country before open strife broke out.

What else could he do but comply? He did not want to fight these people. They had been his neighbors. But where could he go? He would lose his fields, of course. His flocks and his herds were mobile riches; he had wandered lands before and he could do so again, he supposed. But it would not be the same. He could find pastures somewhere, but water was another matter. Sheep and goats needed water to survive, and it had to be dependable water. Many of the wadis carried rushing torrents in the rainy season, and their runoff could offer deceptive hopes to build upon. They could dry quickly and wither away as quickly as they overflowed. He needed dependable sources that could bring him through the dry times, sources that reached down and tapped the everlasting springs deep within the earth. Then he remembered the valley outside Gerar. There had been wells there at one time. They had been good wells, too. His father had dug them, and they had yielded good water. The Philistines had filled them with stones long since because they did not want someone else settling there. The Philistines were farming people themselves, usually staying in the plains to the west, but they had wanted no potential enemies close at hand. So they had stopped up the wells. But water came from deep within the earth, and where there had been water before, there may be water now.

So it was that Isaac had sent his herdsmen eastward with some of his slaves to begin the redigging of the wells. Now his ponderous caravan moved to join them, some three days journey to the east. Three days, that was, for the slow-moving band that carried his wealth. He could have made the journey in one day traveling alone. The temporary camps brought back memories of the more nomadic days with his father, but he discovered that leaving what was familiar that you had chosen yourself was not as easy as leaving what you felt was more or less of others' choosing. That, he thought idly, was probably why revolutions were mostly a product of youth. It was not that youth were really so much more open to change as it was that youth had not yet become accustomed to something long enough to regard it as change. Only those who have become accustomed to something can be said to be faced with change; for others it is only novelty.

Isaac was surprised at the beauty of the place when they finally arrived. A bit of nostalgia tugged at him as he recognized some of the landmarks from his childhood. Why had they left here? He supposed that he simply had not recognized what he was leaving. Water is no different from many other things that are valued little when readily available. He had not known what it meant to be without water before; now, what had been so taken for granted was earnestly sought after, and that made all the difference.

Neglect and abuse had packed the wells so tightly with debris that digging them out was almost as difficult as the task of digging them in the first place. It was hard work, but they were encouraged by the knowledge that others had dug here before and had been rewarded for their labors. It was a day of rejoicing when his servants came to him, dirt-covered, but smiling through their dirt and sweat to announce that they had found water. They handed him a gourd of water, and Isaac drank again of the well that his father Abraham had dug so long ago.

It was a strange feeling to drink this water. He couldn't call it his father's well, because his own servants had had to work as hard as Abraham's servants before them. But while he had had to make it his own, it was also to some degree a gift. He, at least, had known where to dig, and that was no small matter.

Isaac's satisfaction was short-lived, however. There were other herdsmen near the valley of Gerar, and soon conflicts between them and his own servants sprang up. One day his chief herdsman came to him and asked how far he could go in protecting his flocks and the water supply. Could he kill the attackers if he had to protect what was theirs?

"Is it that bad?" he asked. When assured that it was, Isaac shook his head. "No. We will move again."

Even before the move could be accomplished, strong words were exchanged and a few blows were struck; fortunately, no one was killed. Once again the great tent was struck and folded and the great caravan loaded onto the camels. Once again they sought a place where his father had dug a well, and once again they found water. Isaac had named the first well "Contention," and he soon discovered that the appropriate name for the second was little better because strife broke out there also. So he named the second well "Enmity" and moved still farther east.

His third location was more successful, so he called it

"Broad Places" because, at last, there seemed to be room enough for all. But still again he moved. He could not quite explain it, but somehow coming back to old wells reminded him of some of the other things that had been his father's that he had left behind.

Isaac had never really rebelled against his father, nor for that matter against his father's God. He had just come to ignore God and had gone his own way these past years, much as he had with the wells. Other water had been available, and he had not thought that he needed these. Now he found himself wondering if he might have left some other things of value here besides the wells. He found himself more alone than he remembered feeling before. Losing his land and the wealth that it represented and what he had thought was a secure position had done something to more than his personal fortunes. He felt an emptiness inside that was deeper than the material losses. How had his father stood all those years of wandering with only a promise to sustain him? True, he had been told that his descendants would be as numberless as the sands of the desert. But there had been twenty-five years of childlessness before Isaac was born, and his father had been a hundred years old by then! He could still remember his father's voice as he repeated God's call to him: "Go from your country and your kindred and your father's house to the land that I will show you. And I will make of you a great nation, and I will bless you, and make your name great, so that you will be a blessing. I will bless those who bless you, and him who curses you I will curse; and by you all the families of the earth shall bless themselves." And he had gone, not knowing where he went. Isaac remembered the names: Haran, Bethel, and Ai, southward then, even into Egypt, then back again to

Bethel and finally to Gerar. How had he stood it? No perma-
nent dwelling place, a pilgrim and a wanderer wherever he
went, finally buying a cave at Machpelah so he would have a
place to bury his beloved Sarah—but nothing of his own.
Now his bones lay with hers, placed there by Isaac and
Ishmael.

Maybe it was the worship, Isaac thought. Maybe that was
what had kept his father faithful through the years; something
that reached down to everlasting sources like the wells at the
valley of Gerar. There had been other altars, too, he remembered. Perhaps there was a kind of water there that would
quench the deeper thirst that he sensed within himself of late,
even as the redug wells now watered the flocks after their
years of neglect. Strange that he had never thought of that
before. No, not really all that strange. The wide world beck-
ons, other springs sparkle, and horizons call, and old water
doesn't seem to taste as good as others claim it does. So off we
go in search of other wells.

So it had been with Isaac. But now the old springs offered
more than he remembered. Perhaps the wells of worship
could be redug as well. Perhaps he could renew the covenant
that God had made with his father and make it his own. Once
again the black tent was folded and the camels packed, and
the slow-moving herds picked their way eastward. It was to
higher land that they traveled now, for Isaac remembered that
it had been the high places where his father worshipped most.
The journey reminded him especially of the one fearful trip
that he had taken with his father while still a young boy. It was
to a high place that they had gone that day as well, and a
shudder went through him as he recalled it. There were still
times when a ram bleating in a certain way caused the whole

scene to flash before him—the journey, his growing fear, the altar, the upraised knife, and then the bleating of the ram and that awesome voice!

Once again his servants dug for water. While they searched for water, Isaac searched for something else. In the night a voice came to him in the darkness: "I am the God of Abraham your father; fear not, for I am with you and will bless you and multiply your descendants for my servant Abraham's sake." A calmness came to him then that he had not known since they had left Gerar. He had found more than his father's well; he had found his father's God.

The following day Abimelech came to him from Gerar, along with a captain of his army and a friend. At first he thought they came to demand that he move still farther, but he had resolved that he would not. To Isaac's surprise, however, they came in peace, proposing a covenant between them that would bind them in peace.

Isaac was overjoyed, and they sealed their pledge with a meal together. Even as they celebrated, a servant came with the message, "We have found water!"

Isaac smiled as he tasted the water that the servant handed him. It was good water that they had found here, and he named the well Beersheba, "the well of the oath."

2.

WATER FROM BETHLEHEM

1 Samuel 22:1, 26:11; 2 Samuel 23:13-17; John 4:14

David stood at the mouth of the cave at Adullam and held a goatskin filled with water. It was hard to believe that so small a container could hold so much! Not water; memories.

The armies of Saul searched the forests for him, and the king's informers whispered where he could be found. It was probably only because so many different locations had been suggested that he had been able to escape for so long. He smiled at that. Starting his own rumors had not been a bad idea. He continued to marvel at the speed at which the rumors traveled and the ingenuity with which they were expanded upon. Sometimes he could hardly recognize the stories when they came back to him—how many soldiers he had, where and when they had been seen, where they were going, what condition they were in. It was incredible. Being seen and heard of everywhere was the next best thing to being seen and heard of nowhere! As long as there were so many specific places to look, the searchers did not bother to get too systematic about their search. And those who did not travel left no tracks.

But David had about used up all his tricks. He had played the madman to the King of Gath and played upon family loyalties to the king of Moab, but he had carefully kept his base of operations from all except his father and his brothers. He knew that his whereabouts was safe with them. Saul would not risk angering their many friends by trying to torture information on his hiding place from them. People might stand for the killing of David as a rival to the throne, but torturing a family that had been loyal to the kingdom as his father had been would not be tolerated. He was safe for a little while yet. Safe and with a skin of water in his hand. What more could a refugee in the wilderness ask for but shelter and water?

But this was more than water. This was water from the well at Bethlehem, his father's city, the village of his birth. There is something about the taste of water from the springs of home that no one can ever forget. It is a taste that is enriched by the whetted thirst of scratching in your own fields, of tending your own flocks, of working with your own flesh and blood beside you. Fresh dipped, such water always seemed to set your teeth on edge, so cold and good it was. Some might say that a cup of water was a cup of water, but those were they who had always drunk from common wells or who had never been denied the wells of home. Memory makes more precious that which we no longer have.

Water from the well at Bethlehem! Would he ever drink there again? Three men had risked their lives to bring this water to him. The Philistines held Bethlehem now. Jesse, his father, and his brothers were elsewhere, and the city he had loved and called home was a fortress of the hated Philistines.

This was about as far east as he remembered them coming. The Philistines preferred the fertile valleys and the lush hills of Elah and the western plains. They probably would not stay too long because they were too far removed from supplies and reinforcements and their feared war chariots were not as effective in this rough hill country. But they were there now, and the men who had slipped and fought their way through their lines to fill a skin of water were surely foolish to risk their lives in such a way. He had not even known that they were gone, much less where they had gone. He had been more than a little weary of running and hiding and was thinking of his own misfortunes and remembering the pleasures of earlier years as he dipped a drink from the camp water jar.

"Oh, to drink again of the water from the well at Bethlehem!" He was not even aware of saying it aloud at the time, but evidently he had, because here he was, holding the water in his hand. Adino, Eleazar, and Shammah. Three of the bravest of the brave! But to risk their lives for a skin of water? How foolish! Then he stopped himself. It wasn't water that sent them there any more than it was really water that he had wanted. It was love that sent them forth, through the valley of Rephaim where part of the Philistine army was encamped, past the patrols and guards to the very gates of the city where the main Philistine force was garrisoned, and then back by the same hazardous route. It was love and devotion that sent them forth, and it moved him deeply.

What had he really wanted from Bethlehem? He thought a moment, and the answer was clear. What he had really wanted from Bethlehem was what the water reminded him of—an end to running and hiding, the return of peace, the friendship of family and home. Bethlehem was a symbol of so much that was missing now. It was a reminder of so many fine things that had been begun but never completed.

More things were begun in Bethlehem than his life. It was there that the old priest Samuel had come on that unforgettable day and, after watching his seven brothers pass before him, had asked if there was not another son. Being the youngest, David had been tending sheep on the hillsides south of the city when he had been called by his fatner. There, to the astonishment of his brothers and Jesse, the priest took a ram's horn of oil from his belt and poured it over David's head, saying, "This is the Lord's anointed." A strange inner surge of power had seemed to touch him then, and while he did not know then, or yet, all that it meant, it gave him a sense of destiny that he could not quite explain. Some thought him foolhardy and reckless in the days that followed, but it was really more that his time of greatness lay ahead of him and that the seeming difficulties of the moment should not be permitted to stand in the way.

That had been his feeling that day in the valley of Elah when he slew the giant Goliath. He had gone to the scene of the battle at the orders of his father, not to be a part of the fighting but to carry some cheese and a measure of grain and some loaves to three of his brothers who were in the army of Saul. Hearing the challenge of the enemies of his nation had angered him so that he did not really think of the consequences. It was not Israel who was being insulted, he thought, but Israel's God. The nation that won did not simply have the strongest legions, they had the strongest god. And the conquered people usually became converts to whatever religion came with the conquerors. He would not stand by and let his God be so maligned. His victory that day had been the beginning of the bitter jealousy that Saul carried in his heart against him. It was not that David made outward moves against the throne, but the people began to sing their songs, "Saul has slain his thousands, and David his ten thousands." His victory brought him fame, but it also brought him the enmity of Saul. Jealousy is a vengeful master, and no matter how close a friendship he had with Jonathan, Saul's son, no matter that he married one of the king's daughters, and no matter that the music of his harp soothed the savage moods that plagued Saul so, Saul had become his sworn enemy. Twice Saul had nearly impaled him with a javelin while he played his harp. He would never be safe as long as Saul lived.

Yet he could never bring himself to kill his king. Twice he had had the opportunity to do so undetected. Once he had been hiding in a cave similar to the one where he now hid, and the king had entered to spend the night after a fruitless day of pursuit. David's presence was not discovered, and the king lay down to sleep. During the night David crept close and cut a piece from Saul's robe and slipped away. Later he had shown the piece of material to the king to prove that he would do him no harm. It had helped for a while. But the harm that Saul feared from David was not from a knife thrust in the darkness. It was the praise of the people and the fact that Samuel had said that the Spirit of the Lord had passed from Saul to David; soon David was running again.

The second time he had spared Saul's life he and Abishai, one of his men, had crept into the king's camp. His companion had wanted to impale the king with the spear that was stuck in the ground beside him as he slept, but David had refused. Taking the spear and the water jug that was beside Saul's head, they slipped away.

Remembering the water jug caused him to look again at what he held in his hand. Water was precious in this country. It was semi-desert much of the year; without water one did not do much or last long. A person could have many things, but if there was no water, it came to little. David thought again of the bravery of the three men and the tide of memories this water had brought him. Suddenly he knew that there was something here more precious even than the water. This was memory and promise and devotion and all the finer things that made life worth living.

Water from Bethlehem! Would that it could water the whole earth! Would that it could make people everywhere think of love and peace and the fruits of their own labors as well as cleansing and refreshment. Maybe someday, he thought, someone will discover a water that will give them all those things. If one could drink of such water he would never thirst again. Maybe, he thought, smiling, it will even come from Bethlehem! You would never find any better!

David walked to the altar they had built upon which to offer their sacrifices and poured the water over the stones. Such gifts as this could only be from God.

3.

THE THIRD DAY

Luke 1:26-56; Matthew 1:18-25

It was the third day of the week, and the young woman on her way to the village well was thinking of her approaching wedding. The date was still some months away, but she thought of it often, as any engaged girl did. But each third day brought it especially to mind, for that was the day on which the rabbis of her faith had said that the weddings of virgins should take place.

The rabbis had chosen the third day because that was the day of creation on which God had first created life on the earth, "the plants bearing seed according to their kind and fruit trees bearing fruit, each with seed according to its kind." The third day was also the first time that God had said of creation, "It is good." In fact, according to the Book of Genesis, God had said "It is good" not once but twice on this day, making it a day twice blessed. Every Jewish girl knew that and planned her wedding accordingly.

Mary had been engaged to Joseph for several weeks now. Joseph seemed a kind and understanding man, and his building trade promised a reasonable livelihood for the children that she would bear him. She would be proud to be his wife.

In the minds of some, being engaged was the same as being married and the couples were already sleeping together. But Mary and Joseph were not. She understood that to break an engagement at this point would be the equivalent of a divorce in the minds of people, but there were still those who felt that virginity until the wedding itself was a tradition worthy of observation. Mary was one of those, and Joseph shared her convictions. They would honor in the fullest the rabbis teachings that only virgins could be married on the third day.

Already she could visualize the festivities of that day. The ceremony would be in the evening, for that was when her people believed the day began. In Genesis, God had named the evening first, saying, "It was evening and morning, the first day." There would be a fine feast given by her father for the many friends who would be there. The ceremony would not be over until late, and she and Joseph would be escorted through the village with a long procession of torches, going by as long a route as possible so that everyone could have an opportunity to wish them well. They would have garlands on their heads, and they would wear their finest robes. The feasting would go on for an entire week, and they would be treated as if they were king and queen! Her father might have to borrow money to pay for it all, but he would do so gladly. After all, weddings were great occasions in the life of the whole family. There might be much poverty and hardship all the rest of their life, but on those few days festivity and joy would reign supreme.

All of this went through Mary's mind as she made her way to the village well. She went, as all Jewish women did, twice each day, once in the morning and again in the afternoon. Normally Mary looked forward to these trips to the well because they were times of visiting and sharing the latest word that someone might have from family or friends from one of the larger towns. Nazareth was so small. Nothing ever seemed to happen here! Today, however, she went much later than usual. All the other women had already finished their task and their visiting and had returned to their homes. She could see the path ahead of her, and it was completely deserted now. But she didn't mind being alone; she liked the quiet of the evening and the chance to be by herself for a few moments.

It was nearly an eighth of a mile from the little cluster of houses that comprised the village to the grove of bushes and small trees that marked the well site. It was greener around the well because the water that spilled from the women's jars and seeped underground provided extra moisture for the thirsty soil and helped plants to thrive there better during the dry season. Below the well, on the terraced hillsides, were stands of fig and olive trees and the small garden plots that provided most of the income and most of the food for the families who lived nearby.

It was the sixth month, the season of the harvest, but the fields were empty now. The men who tended the trees were already in their homes, preparing for bed, since their main light was from the sun. They had olive oil from their trees, of course, but many could not afford to use it for their own homes. They needed the income it would bring to buy the other goods that they needed and could not grow themselves. They saved a little for times of special need or celebrations, but their bedtimes usually came with darkness. You could tell the homes of those who were more wealthy by the fact that they stayed up later burning oil!

There would be few lights for very long in Nazareth. Nazareth was one of what their prophets had called the "daughter cities," those with no walls to protect them from enemy attacks and with no fighting force of any size to defend them. They called them "daughters" because in the minds of many they were regarded as dispensable and not too important—just as girl children were. Mary's village could barely afford a synagogue, and there were days when the required ten males were not present and they could not read from the Torah. But they had their synagogue; a small one, to be sure, but still a place where the Law could be studied and where her children would learn the Law and the traditions of her people.

Mary thought for a moment of the poverty of her people. The nearest walled city was several miles away—too far to reach in time for protection after any warning they were likely to receive about coming invaders. They had no one to spare who could serve as a scout to give them advance notice of the enemy; all the men were needed in the fields. Even if they were warned and reached a larger city, they may not be let in. Their presence would mean more people for whom to provide food and water if a siege should come. Those inside the walls would simply ignore their cries and use the brief respite their feeble efforts at resistance would provide to strengthen their defenses. "Daughters" were expendable.

One did not have to worry about invaders now, however. The invaders were already here. The town of Sepphoris, only a few miles away, was a Roman garrison. Oh, how the Romans were hated and resented here! Every once in a while one of the young men of the village would slip away to join the Zealots in one of their mountain fortresses in hopes of harassing Rome; and many who did not go in body were with the Zealots in spirit. The whole region was a tinderbox of resentment. Someday it would burst into flames.

The smaller villages seemed to have the hardest times in that the Roman officers did not feel the need to be so careful in how they exercised their authority. Any local resentment could be handled rather easily, they thought. So even though they knew the eagles and other images violated the Jewish religious laws, they never bothered to remove them from their standards when they entered the city. And the soldiers had no hesitation about laying their packs on Galilean shoulders for the required mile of help that Roman law said was due them. Journeys of any distance were complicated and made more expensive by Roman tax booths at the borders of each province. You were taxed going and coming, and you could never be sure what the tax would be until the collector told you. If the collector had not made as much as he wanted that day, the tax could be more coming back than it had been going. That was why the people hated tax collectors so much. In addition to working for the hated Romans, they often oppressed their own people.

A small herd of goats rounded the corner of the slope below her. They were being herded along swiftly now with the growing dusk. They were headed for a cave where they would spend the night safe from animals and thieves. Their herder, for all his haste, was careful to keep them from the garden areas. Sheep could be permitted to graze beneath the trees because they ate only grass and their droppings would enrich the soil. But the goats were browsers and nibbled the ends of the branches and hurt the trees. The goats were also stubborn and had to be driven; they would not follow like the sheep. Still, they were liked and needed for what they added to the food supply of the village. Even now some of their milk and cheese would be cooling in the cavelike storage area dug into the hillside in back of her house.

Mary looked at the zig-zag of the rock fences that served as terrace walls below her. They looked like some giant fish net that had captured the land. Indeed, they did serve as something like a net, keeping the soil from washing into the richer valleys below as so much of it had already done over the years. She had helped to build and repair some of those walls, and she knew what the roughness of the stones did to hands and what their weight meant to arms and backs. But it had to be done; they were poor people, and they needed everything that the land could produce.

Life was hard here in the hills. The fields had to be cleared of stones and terraces had to be built to hold the soil; there was often water to be carried to the trees and gardens. It was grinding toil, and yet Mary shuddered to think how the people of the fertile valleys often paid for their easier lives. The lowlands were the highways of the armies, and the battles for the fortressed cities usually resulted in death or slavery for the residents. Hill people could sometimes escape into the mountains. And while it meant the loss of homes and fields, they at least could keep their lives—sometimes.

Each day Mary prayed that Messiah would come and deliver her people from their bondage. Sometimes she even prayed that she might be the one who would bring such a child into the world. It was mostly fantasy, of course. What woman did not dream of greatness for her children? But after all, the right blood did flow in her veins. Was she not a descendant of

David, the great King? And was not Joseph her betrothed, also of the house of David? And did not the scriptures say that Messiah would come from David's line? The prophet had written:

> There shall come forth a shoot from the stump of Jesse, and a branch shall grow out of his roots.
> And the Spirit of the Lord shall rest upon him, the spirit of wisdom and understanding, the spirit of counsel and might, the spirit of knowledge and the fear of the Lord. And his delight shall be in the fear of the Lord.
> He shall not judge by what his eyes see, or decide by what his ears hear;
> but with righteousness he shall judge the poor, and decide with equity for the meek of the earth.

How they needed such a deliverer now, Mary thought! She smiled a bit at her dreaming. Here she was, not even married yet. Their betrothal had to last for a year, and they had been engaged only a few weeks!

Sometimes Mary wondered if, when Messiah came, he might try a different way than the bloody ways that had been tried before. Was it wrong to wish that Rome could be won without the bloodshed that brought so many deaths? Perhaps she was dreaming, but surely she was not wrong. Death to enemies had clearly been the way for centuries, but it had not brought shalom. Shalom meant more than an end to fighting; it meant wholeness and health and peace for everyone, not just prosperity for the victor and misery for the vanquished.

Might not God try another way next time? She knew that some would say that her wish was only the softness of women, that she did not understand about such things. But she also knew that that was not true. Women had as much strength as men; it was just that their strength was usually applied to different things. For that matter, women could be as hard and cruel as men. Had not Jael, the wife of Heber the Kenite, driven a tent peg through the skull of Sisera, the commander of the Canaanite forces, while he slept in her tent, thus fulfilling the prophecy of Deborah that the Lord would deliver Sisera into the hands of a woman? No, it was not a matter of men or women; it was a matter of how God would choose to act.

Mary's thoughts had slowed her footsteps, and in the dusk of evening the houses of the village were etched against the rose-colored clouds that were the parting gift of the sun. Some birds of evening trilled from the bushes near the well, and overhead a nighthawk called as it skimmed the evening sky for insects. From the village came the voice of a parent calling a child from some last-minute play outside the house. The Romans could not take this from them, she thought: the beauty of creation, the loveliness of the land, their love of God, God's promise to deliver them! She whispered part of one of the psalms as an evening prayer:

> Blessed be the name of the Lord
>   from this time forth and for evermore!
> From the rising of the sun to its setting
>   the name of the Lord is to be praised!
> The Lord is high above all nations,
>   and his glory above all the heavens!
> . . . .
>
> He raises the poor from the dust,
>   and lifts the needy from the ash heap,
> to make them sit with princes,

with the princes of his people.
He gives the barren woman a home,
        making her the joyous mother of children.
Praise the Lord!

Suddenly, Mary's mood of reflection was broken by the sight of a figure near the well. There had been no one there a moment ago, and no one had been nearby. She had made a note of that as she walked. What could it mean? She was a woman alone, and it was getting dark. Should she call out while she had a chance?

The figure spoke before she could make up her mind. "Greetings, most favored one. The Lord is with you."

The words and something in the tone of the voice somehow kept her from real terror, but she felt the stirrings of a different emotion. What kind of greeting was this? What could such a visitor mean? Once again, before she could voice her concerns, the figure spoke.

"Do not be afraid, Mary, for God has been gracious to you; you shall conceive and bear a son, and you shall call his name Jesus. He will be great, and will be called the son of the Most High. The Lord God will give to him the throne of his father David, and he will reign over the house of Jacob forever; and of his kingdom there will be no end."

Overcome with awe, Mary slipped to her knees before what she now knew to be an angel. "How can this be?" she asked. "I have never been with a man. I am still a virgin."

"I am Gabriel," the angel answered. "I stand in attendance upon God, and I have been sent to tell you that the Holy Spirit will overshadow you. Therefore the child to be born will be called Holy, the Son of God."

For a moment Mary could not move. Thoughts poured through her mind. Shock, awe, wonder, joy, hope all mingled together and rushed over her. In her heart a voice seemed to whisper:

My soul magnifies the Lord,
and my spirit rejoices in God my Savior,
for he has regarded the low estate of his handmaiden.
For behold, henceforth all generations will call me blessed.

Slowly Mary rose to her feet, a simple peasant girl in the plain robes that had dressed her ancestors since the time of David. Standing with arms outstretched and palms turned outward, having nothing to offer but herself, she made her answer:

"Here I am. I am the Lord's servant. As you have spoken, so shall it be." No sooner had she spoken than the angel vanished.

For a moment Mary stood beside the well, her water jar forgotten beside her. What would the people of the village say? Her marriage to Joseph was still nearly a year away. A child conceived now would be born before the wedding date arrived. What would Joseph say and do? Would he still take her as his wife? Would he put her aside, divorce her, and bring shame to her father's house?

Then, with a confidence she could not explain, Mary dismissed her fears. Somehow she knew in her heart that Joseph would understand and accept the honor that was to be hers. Somehow, too, she knew that they would still be married on the third day.

4.

A VIEW FROM THE DITCH

Luke 10:29-37

Levi regretted his decision to travel alone almost as soon as he had made it. By the time he left the outskirts of Bethany on the eastern side of the Mount of Olives ridge, he was sure he had made a mistake. For a while he debated turning back to Bethany and hiring a guard or two to accompany him, but he knew no one in Bethany and was afraid that he could end up hiring a spy for the very robber bands that he feared. He had heard of that happening. Besides, one or two guards probably wouldn't make that much difference against a determined group of thieves. They would only serve to advertise that he had something worth guarding. He should have waited until some rich merchant with a large escort was going his way and asked to join the caravan.

Yes, he concluded, he had made a foolish decision. They did not call this road from Jerusalem to Jericho "The Bloody Way" for nothing! The sharp curves in the road, with the steep wadis cutting into the sides and the rough wilderness of Judea so nearby, made ideal hiding and escape routes for the thieves, many of whom were part of the Zealot bands who harassed Rome. And they believed that travelers with money were their legitimate victims, presumably on the premise that they must be collaborators or they would not have any money to steal. Levi had some sympathies for the Zealot cause; he did not care much for Roman occupation either, but the wild life of the Zealots seemed to attract followers who were more interested in the robbing and the booty than the cause. But the Zealots were so obsessed with finding a way to defeat Rome that they did not care how it was done or who helped them do it. At least, that was how it seemed. At any rate, he wasn't interested in getting robbed, even if it was for what might be a good cause! He clutched his staff a bit tighter and hurried on. He had made a bad decision, but he would have to make the best of it.

The two burros moved faster under his prodding, their hooves raising little puffs of dust that swirled and then settled back to earth except when one of the breezes rising from the lower valleys caught them and drifted them like haze across the hillsides. They were both loaded with trade goods, but their travel was much easier now than it had been when they had labored up the same road a few days earlier, laden with produce from the fields and groves of Jericho to be sold in the markets in Jerusalem. Levi could never get used to the difference the elevation made in the weather in the two cities this time of year. It was less than twenty miles, but the difference in elevation plus the warm winds from the desert that warmed the oasis of Jericho meant that it could be snowing in Jerusalem while he gathered produce and citrus in Jericho. That sometimes meant a cold trip, but it also meant good prices for the products he brought from Jericho.

Levi thought of the profit he could make on the load of goods he was bringing back from Jerusalem. He had decided to assign them to a caravan going north to the Greek cities of the Decapolis and the cities of Samaria. These were places that as a devout Jew he would not visit himself, although he had no aversion to making money from them if it could be done through someone else's contact. The caravan owners who traveled from Egypt up the Jordan Valley to the valley of Esdraelon and westward to the shore of the Mediterranean usually had no such aversions to contacts with either the Greeks or the Samaritans, but a good Jew would not enter the cities of either. They shunned the Greek cities because of the idols and statues to the pantheon of gods and the statues of the Roman emperor that were to be found there. The aversion to the cities of Samaria was something else. For Samaria was reserved the intense dislikes that seemed destined to families that had fallen out. Samaria and Judah had once been one kingdom. At the death of Solomon the kingdom had divided, and the bitterness had never healed. To make matters worse, when the northern kingdom of Samaria had fallen to the Assyrians some seven hundred years earlier, the people had been deported and had intermarried with their captors until they no longer had any claim to the Jewish faith. Samaritans were the descendants of settlers imported by the Assyrians to settle the territory after the original inhabitants were deported. At least that was the opinion of the people of Judah.

The Samaritans had a different story. According to them, the deportation was never complete, and many remained in the land. Furthermore, they said, others who were deported were permitted to return about fifty years later. Furthermore, they maintained that Moses had said that the chosen place of

God was Mt. Gerizim, not Jerusalem; and they had tried to stop the rebuilding of the temple in Jerusalem under Ezra and Nehemiah. They called themselves "the observant ones," holding the view that it was the southern kingdom of Judah that was apostate.

Whichever view was correct, Jews and Samaritans had no dealings with each other. Whenever a Jew went north to Galilee, he would travel down this road to Jericho, cross the river Jordan, and travel up its east bank and cross back again after he had passed the northern end of the borders of Samaria. Levi thought of this as he plodded along, recognizing that he could probably make a greater profit if he went himself to those cities instead of assigning his goods on commission to a middle man. But not even for added profit would he go into Samaria. His law taught that if even the shadow of a Gentile or a Samaritan fell upon him, he had to purify himself before he could enter the temple courts to worship. Besides, he did not want to submit himself to the humiliation he might encounter there. The feelings were not at all one-sided. He had heard of Samaritans following a Jew out of their city, dropping straw in their footprints, and setting fire to it. Purifying the land, they said! No, not even for profit would he go there.

Thinking about his safety pulled his thoughts back to the road that he traveled. The countryside was beginning to feel the touch of spring here. The sides of the hills that received the larger amount of sun were showing a faint carpet of green responding to the winter rains; the sides to the north were still brown and barren looking. It made a stark and beautiful contrast. Here and there the brilliant reds of anemonies graced the slopes; and where some bit of underground moisture seeped to the surface, an almond bush was already in bloom. They were one of the first blossoms of spring, but it would be another month before there was dependable grass for the bedouin groups to bring their sheep back into the area.

He was in one of the more dangerous sections of the road now, about halfway between Bethany and the inn that marked the halfway point of a Jerusalem-bound journey. Travelers coming up usually spent the night there because the journey was so much more difficult going in that direction. Maybe he should lay over there tonight and hope for company to go the rest of the way tomorrow.

Rounding a sharp curve of the road, his heart nearly stopped. A small landslide blocked a narrow section of the road ahead of him. Dirt and boulders made the road impassable until some of them could be rolled away. Frightened, he looked about him. He could see nothing but rocks and hillsides. Nothing moved, and no sound came to him. High overhead some bird of prey circled on motionless wings, searching the land for some luckless victim. Did robbers lurk even now in some hidden spot, ready to pounce upon him as an eagle upon a hare? He searched the hillsides again. There were no hiding places that he could see, so after a moment he began to breathe a bit easier. The slide could not have been very recent, he thought, or he would have heard some of the boulders rolling down the side. He could see marks in the lower edge of the road where some had gone on over the steep slope into the valley below. It would take him a little while to clear the road, but it had to be done if he was to continue his journey.

Tying his burros to a small bush, he bent to the task. He found it relatively easy at first to roll a few stones near the edge over the steep side, but he soon realized that he was not in shape for this kind of work. Perspiration streaked his tunic and dripped from his face, some of it running into his eyes and making them smart from the salt and dust. He found himself stopping to catch his breath and wipe his brow more often than he liked to admit. His heart seemed to be racing much faster than he ever remembered. Was it only the exertion and the heat he was working up? Was the temporary energy of fear wearing off? Perhaps that was why the first few stones had rolled so much easier.

He was sitting on a boulder resting a moment, having cleared almost enough to get past when a sound caused him to look behind him, up the road from the direction he had just come. His heart had been racing, but now it almost stopped. He knew they were robbers the moment he saw that there were so many of them and that they carried no packs or bundles, just the short swords and long staves similar to his own. There were nearly a dozen of them, and they came with a look on their faces that he did not like. He suddenly had the feeling that more than his load of trade goods might be at risk.

They were upon him before he could do any more than wonder if he could fight them off. The thought was a foolish one since his own sword and staff were several feet away where he had put them to be out of his way while he worked. His instinctive move towards them was even more foolish. One of the men whirled a sling and a large stone struck him in the chest with considerable force; another grazed his head. He fell in the dust, and soon rough hands were pulling at his cloak and the moneybag tied to his belt. He felt himself rolled over a time or two and thought for a moment that they were going to push him over the steep slope into the valley below.

But for some reason they rolled him the other way, against the bank on the upper side of the road where the run-off of the winter rains had made a shallow ditch. One of the long staves cracked against his arm, and he thought he heard the bone snap. Another struck his head, and everything went black.

He didn't know how long he lay there before he became conscious again. It was the cold that awakened him. He was still in the ditch. The robbers were gone; so were his animals and his money bag and his robe. He was nearly naked, and the coolness at this elevation was rapidly penetrating into the core of his body. He could see that he had bled a good deal, too.

He tried to get to his feet, but he was too weak even to move. One leg was terribly bruised; they must have struck him several times after he passed out, he decided, because he did not remember that blow. The pain in his chest when he tried to move or breathe deeply suggested that he might have a broken rib as well. He knew that he could die here if he did not get help. The loss of blood and the exposure, especially with the coming cold of the night, could easily finish what the robbers had started.

He tried again to pull himself up, but the arm he remembered being struck was useless. He was sure it was broken, and the pain in his side came again. The shock was wearing off, and the pain was beginning. His tongue felt swollen, and his mouth was as dry as the dust in which he lay. He felt a wave of nausea sweep over him, and then the blackness came again.

He didn't know how long he was unconscious this time, but he thought it was a shorter period because the sun did not seem to have changed its angle very much. It was a sound that awakened him this time. At least he was aware of the sound as soon as he was awake. For a moment he thought the robbers were coming back, and the panic almost caused him to pass out again. Then he recognized that the voice was reciting scripture. It was one of what they called "the Songs of Ascent," used by people going on pilgrimage to Jerusalem.

> I was glad when they said to me,
> "Let us go to the house of the Lord!"
> Our feet have been standing within your gates, O Jerusalem!

Suddenly the voice stopped. Levi tried to raise himself again, but he found that he could not move at all now. His eyes were nearly caked closed with the blood from the blows on his head, but he could see through the slits in the lids well enough to make out a man staring at him from several yards away. From his manner of dress Levi knew him to be a priest. Praise be to the Lord! he thought. I am saved.

The man looked around anxiously, his gaze lifting to the higher ground above the road, then back to the wounded man. Why doesn't he come to me? Levi thought. After a moment, he came forward a bit, but he kept to the far side of the road. There was no hurry to his walk, but it seemed obvious that he was going on by.

The next thing Levi knew, he was looking at empty landscape once more. He must have passed out again for a moment. But where was the priest? He tried to twist his head to see more, but the road was empty in both directions. Had the robbers hidden and overpowered the priest, too? Somehow he didn't think so; he felt that the noise would have awakened him even as hurt as he was. Besides, there was nowhere near him to hide. He had seen that when he stopped to move the rocks. The robbers had come from around the sharp bend of the trail that had blocked them from his view, probably having made a big circle through the hills out of sight until they sighted a traveler on the road. Then they would drop in behind him. No, the priest had simply gone on!

Levi was angry. Even his pain was forgotten for a moment. How could someone go on and leave an injured man in the ditch? He felt like cursing at such lack of compassion, and for a moment his mind was filled with anger. After a bit he had another thought. Perhaps the man thought he was dead. He had not been able to call out, and he had not been able to move. There was blood all over his face. He must have looked dead, lying there this way. But couldn't the priest have checked? Couldn't he have come close enough to see if he was breathing, touched him, felt his pulse?

Levi had lived long enough and known enough people to know that one should not expect more of a man simply because he was a priest. He had learned long ago that they were people like everyone else and had the same strengths and failings that everyone else did. But surely the man could have helped a wounded traveler!

For some reason the words the priest had been reciting came back to him. The man was going to Jerusalem, obviously, or at least most likely so. Being a priest, he may have been on his way for a day of service in the Temple. It was a high honor, and some lived out their lives without ever having the lot cast that gave them a time of service there. It was a once-in-a-lifetime opportunity for some. But if a priest touched a dead body, he would be defiled until he could go through ceremonial cleansing. By then his time of service might have passed. That was the Law. Levi knew that, and he had never questioned it before. But now, lying here in the ditch, he wondered if helping the injured might not be a greater service than burning incense in the Temple and if the Law ought not take circumstances into account a little more. Strange how you never think those kind of thoughts until you are the one whom the circumstances effect.

Whatever the cause of the priest's passing by, Levi knew he was in real trouble. If he did not get help soon . . . Suddenly he was hearing sounds on the road again. An animal walking, he was sure of it! A donkey. He had heard that step often enough to know. Again he squinted through his stuck eyelids. He could see the animal now. A donkey with a man riding it! Again he tried to lift himself and succeeded in making a small sound. The rider stopped the donkey at the sound and looked toward him. Levi felt a surge of relief go through him. He had been seen this time, he was certain of it; seen and heard too, so the man could not think that he was dead. His relief was short-lived, however. Suddenly the man kicked the donkey in the ribs and urged him on as fast as the little animal's short legs could carry him, looking frantically up the hillside as he galloped out of sight. The sound of the laboring animal faded in the distance, and the injured man was alone again.

Again he cursed the heartlessness of humanity. Craven cowards who would not help the injured. He knew why this man had gone past; the fear was written plainly on his face as he went by. He was afraid that the robbers were still nearby and that he would be the next victim, even though the hillside had no hiding places. Perhaps he had even thought that the injured man was himself a robber and had covered himself with the blood of some animal in order to lure the unsuspecting near enough to grab them. He remembered hearing how that ruse had worked before, and he recalled his own fear at the first sight of the blocked roadway. Would he have stopped, he wondered, if the situation had been reversed? He could understand the man's fear, but it was little comfort to him lying in the ditch.

Levi's next awareness was the feel of cool water on his face. He felt hands on his body and then the smell of wine and a soothing liquid running into his wounds. Water touched his face again, and he felt the caking over his eyes coming free. Finally he managed to open his eyes; a man was bending over him, his donkey tied nearby. The stranger noticed the opened eyes and quickly placed a drinking spout of waterskin to Levi's mouth. Never had anything tasted so delicious, so refreshing. The water enabled him to find his voice.

"Thank God someone came!" he whispered.

The stranger smiled. "You're badly hurt, but I will put you on my donkey and take you to the inn where I will stay tonight. You'll have help there."

Levi tried to tell him about the robbers, but the man shook his head and told him to save his strength.

"But I have no money to pay the innkeeper," Levi said.

"Never mind," the man replied. "I will pay him and see that you are cared for and guarantee your charges."

"At least tell me your name and where you are from so I can thank you and repay you someday," Levi managed to say.

"My name is Zadok, and I am from Shechem in Samaria."

Samaria! The word struck Levi like a blow. The man who was helping him was a Samaritan! Two of his own countrymen had passed him by, and a despised Samaritan had stopped to help him. He thought a moment of his earlier recital of the bitter hatred between these people and his own nation. If someone had asked him then if he would stop and help a Samaritan along the road . . . well, he didn't like to think what his answer would probably have been.

For the third time in as many hours Levi realized how dramatically one's viewpoint changed when one did his looking from a ditch. And in the days to come as he lay recovering in an inn, he began to wonder if that was not the viewpoint from which God viewed his world.

5.

OPINION POLL IN CAESAREA

Luke 9:54-57; Matthew 16:13-23

How much had they understood, these twelve men that Jesus had chosen after a night in prayer? For nearly three years now he had traveled, eaten, and slept with them. And as time permitted and the Spirit led, he had tried to unfold to them the deeper truths of God. He had tried to begin where they were and teach them, rather than overwhelm them with more than they could understand; but it was very hard! Even these closest friends seemed so slow to understand at times!

Their journey through Samaria had been a revelation. True, he had begun by telling them to go to the house of Israel, to stay away from the cities of the Gentiles. But today he wondered. Sometimes they seemed little more comprehending than the scribes and the Pharisees! On this very journey they had wanted him to call down fire from heaven and destroy a village because the people had not been very hospitable to them. That was bad enough, but remembering that it was a Samaritan village, Jesus found himself wondering how much of the anger was the anger of the moment and how much of it was the deep-rooted prejudices that hurt him so deeply wherever he found them. Anger and resentment were bad enough when they concerned real events in the present. When the present was used to mask the hatreds and prejudices that were so old . . . He shook his head sadly. Would they ever understand?

This was not to excuse the Samaritans, of course. Their prejudices were just as deep. They had denied the little band the traditional hospitality that should have been due any travelers because they recognized them as Jews bound for Jerusalem for the Passover, and the Samaritans had their own customs and holy places. They were as adamant in their ways as the Jews in Jerusalem were in theirs. But to have some of the twelve showing the same ancient prejudices made him ask what his time with them had meant. Was it all for nothing?

His remaining days were few now. The opposition was gathering strength. He would not endorse the status quo of the scribes and Pharisees with their oppressive burdens of the law that buried grace beneath minutia. Nor could he endorse the revolutionary zeal of the Zealots and their cry for blood and violence. He knew that Judas was beginning to resent that refusal more and more. He was loved by many of the common people, but they were not organized like the opposition and they meant little, really, in the politics in which he found himself caught up. He was a man without a base of support. Not that he wanted one, if it had to come at the price of compromising his mission. He had not come to organize some political movement but to try to turn the hearts of all toward God. A platter of promises would have been much easier to sell, but he had rejected that approach on the mountain at the beginning of his ministry.

But he had to know what the twelve had come to believe. He almost dreaded to ask. What if they did not show any more understanding than the rest? Had he been with them all this time without their knowing him? If there was no perception in them, then he had failed, and he might have to stay away from Jerusalem yet awhile longer in order to try again. But if they had caught a glimpse of who he was, then he would be content to face what Jerusalem held for him. But he had to know.

This was an impressionable group, he realized, and often the surroundings in which they found themselves seemed to block their insights into deeper truths, like the incident with the Samaritan village. Or like today. He had been very impatient with them today. He had warned them not to be influenced by the scribes and Pharisees. Using a symbolic reference as he often did, he had said to them, "Beware of the leaven of the scribes and Pharisees." And how had they responded? They had begun to mumble among themselves about how they had taken no bread!

Impatiently, he had rebuked them, saying, "Do you not yet understand? Are you blind with your eyes wide open? Do you have ears that do not hear? Is understanding impossible to you? Can't you comprehend what I am saying? Can't you even remember what your eyes have seen? Why should I be worried about loaves of bread?"

He had asked them then if they remembered how many baskets of fragments they had gathered up after the feedings of the multitudes. How ironic that they remembered the numbers, but could not recall the meaning of his words! Finally it dawned on them that producing bread was not his concern, and they figured out that he was using the influence of the yeast in bread as a symbol for teaching. But he would not always be with them to pull them through so tediously.

If only they could find that central truth and fix upon it, provide some foundation upon which the Holy Spirit could build in the days to come! It had to be there. Surely, they had some comprehension. BUT HE HAD TO KNOW!

Today was to be their test.

He did not want the test to be too easy. Knowing their impressionability, he had taken them to a place where their senses would be surrounded with many memories and influences. He had taken them to Caesarea Philippi. It was a region in the north of Galilee, where there were few Jews and where his opposition and their interruptions would be minimal. He had led them here before. It was a safe retreat from any active hostilities and a good spot for renewal.

It was a beautiful land through which they traveled. Well-watered from the heights of Mt. Hermon, wheat fields and barley fields graced the roadsides. The flowing streams offered refreshment, and the forests of the slopes beckoned with their cooling shade. On other trips he had yielded to such appealing places of rest, but this time he came to answer a deeper call. He had come to such places before to teach; now he came to test.

This was a region filled with religious history. Scattered about them were the shrines of Baal worship from the days of the Syrian occupation. In the distance, on a clear day, you could see the heights of Mt. Carmel where Elijah had challenged their prophets to the famous duel to pray down fire from heaven. The myths of the Greek gods were rooted here as well. Nearby was a great mound in the earth, and beneath the mound was a deep cavern, said to be the home of the nature god, Pan. Here, too, the Jordan river found its life in flowing springs deep within the mountains. Even more, Caesarea Philippi was a center of emperor worship. Herod the Great, father of the Herod now in Jerusalem, had built a great temple out of white marble and dedicated it to Augustus Caesar. You could see its gleaming whiteness in the sun from miles away. If there was any place where the traditions and expectations of the past might shape and color their response, this was the place. If visions of political messiahs still lurked in their minds, these surroundings should bring them out. And while he hoped against hope that he had succeeded in showing them a higher kingdom, he could not let his hopes blind him to reality. What he hoped that they would say was not enough. He had to hear their own responses shorn of his expectations or his dreams. Here they must speak and he must listen.

"Who do men say that the Son of man is?" he asked them suddenly. He had never asked them that before. There were so many expectations heaped upon the word *messiah* that he had refrained from using it, even to the twelve. But they knew full well what those expectations were: freedom from the oppressors, political independence, a return to the glory that was Israel in the days of David. Even many who disagreed on the method by which all of this was to be achieved agreed on the results that they could expect when Messiah came. Some expected God to act in some mighty way; some insisted that they must take up the sword and act themselves. That the disciples were not purged of those kinds of images was clear from some of their own bickering and from the request of Salome, the mother of James and John, that they be given places of honor in the coming kingdom.

Patiently, and sometimes not quite so patiently, he had tried to show them that his way was different. He sought a kingdom of the heart that would indeed change society through changed people who would act in changed ways. Sometimes he thought they truly understood, and sometimes he questioned if they understood at all. But he had pressed on, refusing to fit their molds, resisting the ways suggested even when they were more tempting than when he was in the wilderness. Once he had felt temptation working so strongly through Simon Peter that he had even called him Satan!

But now he put the question to them, starting it from a less threatening direction by asking what others were saying about him.

The answer, when it came, was much what he had expected. "Some say you are John the Baptist, some say Elijah, others say you are Jeremiah or one of the prophets." A sad smile touched his lips as he heard their answer. It was a way in which they could hold on to their messianic expectations and still explain the signs and wonders he had performed. It also denoted a respect for his own ministry. John the Baptist had been a popular prophet to some of the common people because of the zeal with which he had attacked the rich; Elijah and Jeremiah were both said to be forerunners of the Messiah who would return to earth to teach and perform miracles before Messiah came in glory. Jeremiah was said to have hidden the ark of the covenant and the holy vessels someplace on Mt. Nebo, and it was said that he would come and reveal them to inaugurate the coming reign of Messiah. By hailing him as one of those men, they could acknowledge some sense of greatness in him without giving up all the good things that Messiah was supposed to do for them.

Ah, there was the rub! They were more interested in what

Messiah could do *for* them than what he might do *to* them! John the Baptist, Elijah, Jeremiah—it was something, but it was not enough. Not nearly enough. But his real interest was in these twelve. It was their reply that he must have. While he hoped for more from the general public, these twelve were critical. If none of them could see anything more than what he had heard so far, he had failed.

The die was cast now. He would wait no longer. He pressed on with his second question. "But who do you say that I am?" There it was. He found himself almost holding his breath as he waited for their answer. Would they echo the crowds? Here amidst the ruins of ancient competitors of their fathers' God, here in the shadow of the myths of Greece and in the sphere of influence of emperor worship would their thoughts go to the traditional deliverance that was expected by so many? Public opinion, vicariously expressed, would not be enough upon which to build. Personal conviction alone would stand the strain of conflict, the pain of opposition, the challenge of growth. He must know what these men thought.

These men knew him as no others did. Oh, they still wavered and missed the mark at times, but they had grasped *something* of his spirit. They also knew what most people expected the promised Messiah to be and do. The two images were simply not compatible. He knew that, and that was the point of his question. If they saw him as Messiah, then he had won. If they recognized him as God's chosen one, then in the days to come their understanding of Messiah would grow to fit what he was instead of their continually trying to work it the other way. "Who do you say that I am?"

It was no surprise that it was Simon Peter who spoke. He was the outspoken one among them. He would tell you what he thought, and quickly. He did so now: "You are the Christ of God."

Jesus knew then that he had won. He now had the fulcrum with which to move the earth. The Enemy could do what he would; and while there might be hard times and wavering men and women, while understanding might rise and fall, the Holy Spirit would find a dwelling place. The Spirit would find it in Peter and in others who would come to share his testimony. The church would come to be, and the gates of hell would not prevail against it.

6.

NIGHTFALL

John 13:27-30; Matthew 26:1-25

Judas paused a moment in the doorway. Behind him the oil lamps flickered and cast dark shadows against the wall behind the twelve men still reclining on the low couches that filled the center of the room. The corners of the room were dark, being shielded somewhat from the light, but the darkness there was nothing compared to the scene beyond the doorway in which he stood. Beyond the doorway the night appeared to be almost a tangible thing, as if you could touch it or feel it or even squeeze some of the darkness out of it. Blackness seemed to drip from the sky and cover everything; it collected in pools along the sides of buildings and hid even the faintest outlines of structure. There was an ominous quality in this night, and even one who was used to the dark could feel the threat—as if this were the night that would overcome the light and from which the dawn would never escape.

Judas felt the fear and wondered at it. Did the others suspect him? Did they know the dark errand that called him even now? No. That could not be. They could not know that or they would never have let him leave the room. Besides, the way each one had asked the question "Is it I, Lord?" was proof enough that they did not know.

The Master's announcement had burst upon them like a clap of thunder from a clear sky. "One of you will betray me," he had said. It was not a question or even an exclamation. It came as a simple statement, as if Jesus had already come to terms with the fact himself and was resigned to its inevitability. All that had saved Judas was the fact that everyone else seemed to feel the same shock that he did. His own startled expression was little different than those on eleven other faces. Each one seemed to realize that he had failed Jesus before and recognized the possibility of doing so again. Even John had asked if he would be the one. It was when John spoke that Judas knew that he would have to ask also. He could not let it rest that he was the only one who did not feel that possibility, but he had thought that he would never get the words to come out of his throat. His voice seemed strained and strange to his own ears. He thought surely the very sound of it would betray him, but no one seemed to pay him any specific attention. He guessed that each one was too preoccupied with searching his own soul to suspect anyone else. As for himself, he had nearly died when Jesus had looked at him and said, "What you do, do quickly." How did he know? *What* did he know?

For a moment Judas had nearly panicked. The Teacher's eyes seemed to pierce his soul, and he sensed in him a pleading that he could not quite understand. But he was resolute; the deed was already done. The coin purse that he carried at his side was heavy with the coins—thirty of them.

He tried not to think that they represented the going price of a slave in the marketplace, but the irony of it would not leave him. To sell the Master for the price of a slave!

He had been jolted hard when the high priest had counted out the amount that they would pay for what he would do that night. Were they mocking him? Did they know how often Jesus had spoken of the servant role for the Messiah?

It was that attitude of servanthood on Jesus' part that had finally made Judas decide on his course of action. For a long time he had thought that Jesus was only biding his time, waiting for the strategic moment to proclaim himself as the long-awaited One who would throw off the yoke of Rome and restore Israel to its rightful place among the nations. The rich and prosperous upper class who catered to the Romans would be thrown out, and the common people would divide up their estates. Israel would once again be for true Israelites. Yes, it would be grim and bloody for a while, and many would die, perhaps even many of those for whom the revolution was supposed to be waged. But was it not better to die fighting for freedom than to live in slavery?

Those who led the revolution would be the princes of the new Israel, and they would no doubt have to institute their own controls to keep the revolution from getting out of bounds. But then someone had to be in charge; why not them? And why shouldn't he be one of them? Once it had occurred to him that this was exactly how the present puppet leaders no doubt felt, and he wondered if every aspiring rebel rationalized his violence in this manner. But when such thoughts came, he always told himself that it would work out for the best; the end would justify the means.

So he had waited for Jesus to name the moment for the

rebellion. Several times he had almost given up, but each time he had decided to wait a little longer. The events of the past week had brought it all to a head, however. First, there had come the wasted opportunity when the crowds had welcomed them into the city. It would have been a perfect time for Jesus to announce his identity and call for an uprising! Jerusalem was filled with people, as it always was for such holy days. The shouting crowds were worked up to an emotional pitch that would have given an impetus to the day that none other could approach. He could see the more knowing of the Roman soldiers fingering their swords when the people began laying palm branches in the path of the little donkey that Jesus rode. Some of them knew a bit of Jewish history and remembered that crossed palms were on the backs of the coins from the times of the Maccabees, the last period of Jewish freedom. Many of the people placed them that way in the streets. It was subtle enough and filled with political symbolism, but you could hardly arrest people for throwing palm branches. The Pharisees and the Sadducees noted the action, too, and their anxiety was as great as that of the soldiers. They recognized the power of this man, and they feared how he would use it. They knew that any revolution would leave them out of power, and they could not tolerate that. The symbolism of the palms had not been lost on the Master, either. He knew their meaning, but it had only moved him to tears and a sad discourse over Jerusalem's failure to heed the prophets.

It was then that Judas had decided that he had made a mistake. Jesus would never do what Judas was convinced was necessary to right the wrongs that plagued his people. He was a soft Messiah. He talked of a kingdom of God, but he was not willing to fight for it. The day before, while they were resting in Bethany, Judas had seen a penitent woman pour the jar of spikenard over Jesus' feet and had gasped at the waste. When he thought of how many swords and daggers that money would have bought, how many rebels it would have armed for the day that was ahead of them, he had blurted out an objection. He had covered his objection by talking about giving it to the poor in general, but Jesus had quietly rebuked him, saying that they would always have the poor around them and that this woman was anointing him for burial. That statement had ended any discussion of the matter.

The week had gone slowly for him, in spite of the busy schedule of teaching. His hopes had flared again when Jesus had driven the moneychangers from the Temple, but nothing had come of that either, except to anger his enemies more. The anger Jesus had shown so briefly seemed to come from the desecration of the Temple, not from any real opposition to the system. It could have been used to provide a springboard to larger action if Jesus had wanted to pursue the matter, but again the moment passed. It was the pivotal point for Judas, however. He had gone to the chief priests immediately afterwards. He could not stand the thought of such ignoring of opportunities, such waste of resources, such disregard for the poor. At least that was what he told himself. He was also aware that deep down he was angry at himself for having backed the wrong man.

After the deed was done, Judas had tried to tell himself that by putting Jesus in the hands of his enemies, he would force Jesus to use his power to save the cause because he would need it to save himself. But when he was honest with himself, he had to admit that it was simply that Jesus' way and his way were not compatible and that he, Judas, was not willing to change. He did not doubt the Master's love and compassion for the poor. He had seen him heal the sick and feed the hungry; he had seen the energy drain out of him from the hours of teaching and helping. But Jesus always seemed to put spiritual needs above bodily needs somehow. It was as if he felt that the poor could be as turned aside as the rich could by a focus on material things. He seemed to feel that the poor could miss the kingdom by seeking what they didn't have just as the rich could by seeking more. Yet he had heard Jesus tell the rich to share what they had, and even tell some of them to sell their goods and give the money to the poor. What was wrong with telling the poor to demand what Jesus told the rich to give them?

Well, it was done now. He was to meet the guards sent by the high priest and lead them to the place where they could take Jesus without the people being aware of it. He knew where that would be: the olive grove in Gethsemane, across the Kidron valley. Jesus went there often to pray when he was troubled, and Judas knew that he was going there after their meal. No one else would be there, and there should be no trouble at all.

Judas thought of one other bad moment that evening. The disciples had been arguing over which of them would be the greatest in the coming kingdom. James and John had been putting forth their case, and Peter was his usual strong-willed self. Judas had not entered into the argument because he had already decided that there was not going to be any kingdom, at least not the kind that he wanted. But a little later when they had arrived at the room that had been prepared for them and Jesus had indicated that he, Judas, was to sit beside him in the guest of honor position, he had nearly given it up. John was on the other side of Jesus. Simon Peter, indignant at not being invited to sit in either position, had stomped petulantly around and seated himself at what was considered to be the lowest position at the table, acting like a spiteful child who, being refused what he wanted, proceeded to break his favorite toy. Jesus' action was not lost on Judas. He felt the pull of old loyalties for a moment, but it passed. He had made his bargain, and he was not going to ride that peak and valley road again—one moment his hopes high only to have them dashed low the next. What he had done, he had done; and whatever the Master may have meant with his words, "What you do, do quickly," they had firmed his resolve.

Behind him in the room he heard Jesus giving thanks over the loaf and the cup, but there was a difference in the words that he was using this evening. He had never heard him speak of his body and his blood as a new covenant before. He stood silhouetted in the doorway for a moment. The glow of the lamps cast his shadow forward where it was swallowed up by the greater darkness that lay in wait. Then Judas stepped through the doorway and closed the door behind him. The darkness was complete.

7

VERDICTS FROM STRANGERS

John 19:13-42; Luke 23:34-55

They called the hill Golgotha, which in Hebrew means "the place of the skull," because of its domelike shape and the three weather-carved cavities in the face of the exposed rock that resembled the eye and nose sockets of a human skull. The area had been a stone quarry centuries before, but the better stone had long been quarried out and taken away to build some of the better structures of Jerusalem. Perhaps some of the stones of the Temple itself had come from here; or one of the great stones of the city wall. Surely they would have quarried those as nearby as possible.

Later, after the quarrying was finished, the area had become a cemetery. The uneven surfaces and exposed crevices left from the cutting made the beginnings of openings for individual graves and for the larger tombs favored by the richer families of Jerusalem. The area's use as a cemetery went back further than anyone living could remember, even though one family might use the same tomb for generations. Bones from earlier burials were taken from the ledges on which the bodies were originally placed and deposited in a special chamber hollowed out for that purpose in the back of the open area of the tomb. Mixed with the older burial sites were more recent tombs, including some that had not yet been used at all.

The hill was on the western side of the city, just outside the western wall. The cemetery would seem to preclude any expansion of the city in that direction, since the law forbade any dead being buried within the city. But other cities had been destroyed and rebuilt in later years over unknown cemeteries because no one living remembered that the graves were there.

Golgotha was also a garden area. The scarcity of good land in rocky hill country meant that few favorable areas went long without someone putting them to use. Grapevines had been planted in the low-lying areas where the soil had accumulated to adequate depth. The available stone also made good material for presses and for storage vats.

The name "Golgotha" was fitting now for more reasons than the geographical features that caused it to resemble a skull and the social usage as a place of burial. The Romans had chosen the hill as the place where they executed condemned criminals. The most obvious features of the site were the "trees" that the Romans raised as crosses; the grisly fruit they bore was human bodies. This was a place of crucifixion.

Rome's choice of the hill was not rooted in the death's head appearance or in the site's convenience as a cemetery. Rome was more pragmatic even than that. Not far from the rough outcropping of stone was a gate to the city of Jerusalem called the Gehenna, or Judgment Gate, and one of the most heavily traveled roads passed by the spot. Rome wanted the greatest possible impact from its execution of criminals; consequently, they saw to it that crucifixions happened where people would be shockingly reminded of the fate of those who defied Rome. The same desire for maximum impact also decreed that a placard be placed on the cross, naming the crime for which the individual had been condemned. On this day Pontius Pilate had taken special care to see to it that there was no question concerning one of those who hung there. The sign on the center cross read, "Jesus of Nazareth, King of the Jews." It was written in three languages—Hebrew, Latin, and Greek. There were at least two motives in Pilate's action and in his refusal to add the qualifying "This man said he was" that the religious leaders requested of him. First of all, he wanted a clear object lesson to any would-be insurrectionists that this would be the fruit of their actions; but even more, Pilate would have the last word in his bout with those religious leaders.

"What I have written, I have written," he declared in answer to their request, as if to let his stubbornness on this matter atone for his earlier cowardice in refusing to free the man in whom he said he could find no fault.

Mary had heard of Pilate's verdict through the servant communication system that operates so effectively in many large households that it is the envy of every information system in the world. Decisions and pronouncements were often on the street before they were hardly out of the mouths of the speakers. As is often the case, such speed sacrifices accuracy, and Mary had had her hopes raised for a while, only to have them cruelly dashed to pieces by the later word that the political pressures were such that the verdict was meaningless. Under the threat of unfavorable reports to Caesar,

Pilate had gone on to issue the sentence of death in spite of his verdict of innocence.

This seemed to be a day of meaningless verdicts about her son, Mary thought, as she stood on the skull-shaped mound and watched her son suffer. One of the thieves had begun to revile and curse the teacher because he did not use his power to free them all from the sentence of death that was upon them, but the other thief had rebuked the first, declaring that while they were justly condemned for their deeds, this man had done nothing wrong: a second verdict of innocence.

A mother seldom needs others to tell her good things about her son, but what mother does not cherish verdicts from strangers that confirm her own convictions? The irony of the words of the thief, echoing as they did the opinion of Pilate, was not lost on Mary, even in the anguish of this moment. The law required that evidence in a trial be presented by two witnesses, separately examined and without contact with one another, in order for it to be acceptable. One could hardly find two more dissimilar witnesses than Pilate and a condemned thief!

Pilate's verdict had spoken to those who would make Jesus into a revolutionary. The Zealots had tried to enlist him in their cause, and some had been disillusioned when he did not make the procession of palm leaves into an occasion for mobilizing the people into rebellion. Mary had heard the murmurings afterwards, even from some who had been close to Jesus. The religious leaders had charged Jesus with such sympathies only because they knew that was the charge most likely to bring the wrath of Rome most heavily upon him. And Pilate, while he knew their guile and their envy, had to take the charges seriously no matter what he felt about their motives. He dared not free one so charged without being sure of his grounds. To do so was to risk the wrath of Caesar in the worst way. If someone was stirring up the people as his enemies charged that Jesus was doing, Pilate would know. Pilate had to know; his own future depended upon his knowing. When such a man declared Jesus innocent, it had to be because he was convinced that there were no grounds for the accusation at all.

Mary winced inwardly at the thought that some might in later years think that her son was guilty of such crimes as those of which he was accused. That he who had pleaded for love between enemies could be remembered as advocating death and violence toward his nation's enemies would hurt her almost as much as his death was hurting her. She hoped that somehow the world would know of Pilate's verdict. She had never known the man, except by public sentiment and reputation, but suddenly she felt that what he had said in those council chambers needed to be remembered. She vowed to thank the servant girl who had sent the word to her, even though it was not the final verdict of that night: "I find no fault in him." One vote for innocence in the midst of his accusers!

The witness of the thief was a different matter entirely. Obviously his word meant nothing in the proceedings of the day. Perhaps no one but a mother would even have remembered such a word; who cared what a thief had to say?

Mary found herself wondering if on some summer's day when this man had walked a freer path, he might have stood in some crowd on some flowered hillside in Galilee, or on the rabbi's teaching steps outside Jerusalem's southern wall, and heard her son speak of a way of life that was revolutionary— but not in the way that his enemies tried to accuse him. His enemies recognized what he said all too well as a threat to their way of life. But what he had to say could also attract even those who did not follow it if their hearts were not so hardened that nothing could penetrate their shell. The thief was bearing witness to a goodness that was attractive, even though he had turned away. Sometimes those whose paths have taken them in ways such as he had evidently followed can be harsher judges than society at large; they are quick to identify hypocrisy and sham, and they have no patience with those who practice either. For such a man to declare her son innocent was no small thing; he represented the multitudes who heard him so gladly, the outcasts who climbed trees to get a glimpse of him or clutched at the hem of his garment as he passed by.

Two votes for innocence! Little good they could do him now, she thought. He had dreamed of a way without violence and death and had turned away from the shedding of blood, but he was bleeding and dying now.

Mary remembered that most of the Jewish community would share the Passover meal this evening. Jesus and his disciples had observed it by the calendar of the Essenes and eaten the meal earlier in the week. Did it mean anything that an innocent one was dying on a cross as the innocent lambs were being killed in the temple courts in preparation for the evening meal? She realized that Israel would be joyously celebrating its most sacred festival while she was experiencing her great sorrow.

Mary remembered again the words of the angel that had come to her in Nazareth in what now seemed an eternity before: "He will save his people from their sins." She remembered, too, the solemn words of the old one, Simeon, in the temple at the time of her purification after the birth. He had told her that a sword would pierce her own soul through this special life that was destined for so much.

Mary still did not understand what it all must mean. But on a bleak and dismal day, with her son dying on a cross while she stood helplessly by with nothing to offer except her presence, she gathered what comfort she could from the verdicts of strangers, verdicts that confirmed her own convictions.

The sky had grown steadily darker, and a hush settled over the crowds gathered on the hill of the skull. Mary strained to hear some word or sound from the figure on the center cross. He had spoken but little through the long ordeal. Typical of his life, he had spoken of others first: forgiveness for his enemies, an expression of his concern for her future that nearly tore her heart in two, an expression of his own suffering—physical, with his cry of thirst, and spiritual, with his awful cry of loneliness. Would he speak again?

With a mother's special memory she recalled the nights when she had listened in the night, as a mother does, for some whimper of discomfort or distress that others do not hear; sounds that somehow reach a parent's ears. Would he speak again?

In the silence that shrouded the hillside as the sky darkened even more and the earth shook as if in anger, she heard once more the voice that she had come to know so well.

"It is finished. Father, into thy hands I commit my spirit."

It was the confidence in the tone that surprised her most. Somehow it made her think of one of the times that he had been working on some small project and had walked into the room where she and Joseph were talking to announce that he had completed what he had been working on. Gone was the anguish and the pain that had marked his most recent words of thirst and loneliness. He was a child speaking to a caring parent, with a confidence and a trust in his tone that marked a very special relationship.

Mary could not help but remember how that tone of voice in his prayers and talk of God had marked him so early in his life—like the time in the temple when he was twelve and they thought he was lost, only to find him there after three days talking with the rabbis and asking them questions.

"Didn't you know I would be here, about my father's business?" he had asked them, honestly surprised that they had been worried about him. Somehow all through his life he had managed to keep that directness and profundity that most children lose too soon.

In the continued silence Mary heard yet another verdict offered concerning her son; another from as unlikely a source as the two that had somehow offered her some meager comfort on this day.

The centurion who had commanded the detachment in charge of the crucifixion had acted strangely all afternoon. He had let her and John and the two other Marys approach much closer than was usually permitted. Now he spoke seemingly to himself, but the words carried to a mother listening for the slightest sound.

"Truly, this was the Son of God."

A shock went through Mary; a third verdict for innocence on this day. She knew that her son was dead now. His simple statement had made that clearer to her than any cry of pain or gush of blood could ever do. But coupled with her memory of how he had lived out the relationship that he had claimed so naturally, Mary found herself wondering if all the witnesses had really been heard from today after all. She wondered if the final verdict might belong to God.

8.

A CENTURION'S CONVICTION

Matthew 8:5-13, 27:51-54; Mark 15:33-39

Gaius hurriedly led his little band of hand-picked soldiers and their sorry spectacle of a victim through the narrow streets of Jerusalem. His destination was a crossroads just outside the city gates where a rise of ground had been named, appropriately enough, "the place of the skull."

The route they travelled was not the most direct route to that part of the city. Gaius's expectation of no disturbance lay in that fact more than in the number of his soldiers. He would have preferred to have had three times the number he had been assigned, but by his splitting of the forces to send the larger group with the other two prisoners by the usual route, he had hoped to confuse any who might have been thinking of a rescue attempt. His decision was a gamble, but he felt that it was worth it. They would be at the crucifixion site before any would-be rescuers could determine where to strike—if they were going to. Judging from the scattering of the close followers of this teacher, Gaius doubted that they would do anything. The Sanhedrin had acted quickly, and Pilate had lost no time once he saw that a crucifixion was inevitable. There had been little chance to organize any opposition.

Gaius was proud of his rank of centurion. It was a noble office, filled with history and laden with honor. He commanded a hundred soldiers in the army of Rome. While they were responsible to the legionnaire who commanded sixty like themselves, the centurions were really the working officers of the command. A statesman had once said of them that they were not required to be bold and adventurous so much as steady leaders who, when hard-pressed and overwhelmed, would stand at their post and die. Many of them had done just that, and Gaius was proud to be a part of this tradition and the responsibility that accompanied it.

He had risen through the ranks from common soldier not only to centurion, but to "Primus Pilus," the first of ten, senior centurion of the first ten cohorts of the legion. That office was as high as a common soldier could rise in the army of Rome. With that position went some of the hardest jobs—like the one today. If anything went wrong here today, Pilate wanted someone in charge who was responsible enough to take the blame and to keep it as far from his own office as possible. Trust Pilate to see to that!

Pilate would never know how close Gaius came to refusing the task today. He had never refused an order before. For that matter, he had not refused this one when it finally came down to it, but it had been a very close thing. The near-rebellion was rooted in the prisoner who stumbled along beneath the heavy beam of the cross on which he would die.

Gaius had heard this teacher speak and had been impressed by the authority and quiet assurance with which he taught; he was also moved by some of the things he heard the teacher say. But even more, there was the incident of the healing of one of his fellow officer's servants. The story of this healing had been told throughout the officer corps with the speed of gossip. Since the other centurion was a friend, Gaius had made it a point to verify the incident.

It had been in Capernaum, Flavius told him. Flavius had been aware that as a Gentile he had had no claim on a Jewish teacher, and he had gone prepared for a rebuff of some kind, or at least a polite excuse to cover up the dislike and resentment that could be found in so many toward a ranking representative of the conqueror. But he had not been received that way at all! He had been overwhelmed when the teacher had offered to come to his home. Orthodox Jews would not enter a Gentile town, much less a Gentile house. There had been no questions, no hesitation, none of the fleeting expressions of resentment that he had become so adept at recognizing in conquered people, Flavius said. Just a simple statement: "I will come and heal him."

The confidence in that reply had left Flavius stunned for a moment. How could the teacher heal the servant when he didn't know what was wrong? Of course, Flavius had gone asking for help, but he had not been prepared for such assurance. Flavius had told his friend Gaius, "I was amazed. I wasn't worthy enough to have him come under my roof. I said to him, 'Only say the word and my servant will be healed. I am a man of authority. I have men under me, and I say to this one go and he goes, and to another come and he comes. You have but to say the word and my servant will be healed.' "

The teacher had been astonished that Flavius would say

this. Flavius thought that at least he could save the teacher further criticism from those who were complaining because the man ate and drank with sinners.

"He told me to go home, that my servant was healed, and I found it just as he said," Flavius had declared. "In fact, upon inquiring on the hour that the healing took place, I determined that it was just at the time I was talking with the teacher."

It had been Flavius's story that had caused Gaius to listen to some of this man's teachings, and he had come to have a deep respect and admiration for him and for what he had to say. Now here he was in charge of the teacher's crucifixion! What irony of fate had engineered this? He didn't enjoy this work at any time, unlike a few that he knew. It was a job that had to be done, and if he didn't do it, someone else would, perhaps with less caring than he tried to inject into it when he could.

It had been a close thing, that almost refusal, but with retirement only two years away—well, if you wanted to retire in rank, you had to keep your nose clean and do what you were told. To refuse a job would be received pretty hard. Besides, his refusal would not have changed an iota of what was happening here today. If he had felt that it would, it might have been a different matter. All that it would have changed would have been Gaius's future. To put it bluntly, he would not have had much future. Oh, they would not have crucified him; Rome saved that death for common criminals. Internal discipline was dealt with in other ways. The front lines of battle always needed fresh blood, and it was better to let a reluctant officer go back to digging trenches and scaling walls than to be wasted on some grubby garbage heap. No, he would have been quietly replaced and reassigned. A few might have wondered, Whatever happened to Gaius? but by and large the response would have been a momentary scramble for his position and then a return to everything as before. His absence would have been noticed about as long as you notice a hole in a bucket of water when you take out a dipper full.

He found himself wondering what would have happened had Flavius drawn this assignment. Would he have refused? How does one deal with the conflicts between conscience and duty? between conscience and livelihood?

Gaius had received his latest promotion soon after the incident in Capernaum; as was common in Roman army promotions, he had been transferred to another post. He had been sent to Caesarea as first centurion in Pilate's private corps. Now he was in Jerusalem because Pilate was here, and Pilate was here because of the unrest that was so common during the Jewish holy days.

Gaius hated these times! He hated trying to keep two calendars operating in his head, one Roman and one Jewish. He knew his Roman calendar because he was a Roman and proud of it. Roman holidays meant little here, and while the Jewish calendar meant nothing to him personally, it meant everything to his work. The feast days, the special gatherings of pilgrims for what they called their sacred history, added up to more people and more emotion and more potential for trouble. And trouble was his business. The Passover season was the worst of all. Jews came from all across the world. They remembered their deliverance from Egypt centuries earlier with a passion that was almost unbelievable, and the Zealots among them were always comparing Rome to that earlier oppression and implying some new deliverance was imminent. Everyone's nerves were on edge because some seemingly meaningless incident could escalate into a revolution.

Gaius had been afraid of just such an event earlier in the week when this teacher, who some called a prophet, had appeared and crowds of pilgrims had lined the road and thrown palm branches across his path. The slightest encouragement from this man and anything could have happened. It soon became obvious that he had no interest in revolution, at least not the kind of revolution that Rome was concerned about. This recollection was part of why Gaius had so little concern about a rescue attempt now. It was simply not this teacher's way.

Gaius had made a point of reporting all of this to Pilate and had reminded him of it again when the religious leaders came forward with their charges. For a while he thought Pilate was going to free the teacher. How Gaius had hoped for that! The note from Pilate's wife had added to his hope. He was sure it had something to do with this Jesus because of the way Pilate kept looking at his prisoner while he read it. He had never seen Pilate as agitated as he was after that note arrived. The governor had tried again to release the teacher just afterwards, but the religious leaders would have none of it. They wanted this man's life and they were determined to have it. That became very clear. The scourging that Pilate ordered in an effort to elicit sympathy and in the hope that it might appease the religious leaders had only put the poor victim through another ordeal. That was when Gaius decided that there was nothing that he could do. Not even Pilate could save the teacher. What could a centurion do?

Nevertheless, he had tried again to convince Pilate of the prisoner's innocence, but it was not Pilate who needed convincing. He had shrugged his shoulders and called for a basin of water to wash his hands, saying this man's blood was not his guilt. Would that guilt was relieved as easily as that! Pilate's future was on the line and he knew it. He had already pushed these people more than he should have, and Rome took seriously the complaints of local citizens against their governors when they involved matters that threatened the security of the empire. Reasonably contented people were easier to control than angry ones, and it was easier to replace unpopular governors than to put down revolutions.

A clatter on the paving stones caused Gaius to grip his sword and draw it halfway out of its scabbard. He relaxed a little when he saw that it was only the teacher falling again. The scourging had been a bad one, and the loss of blood had weakened him. Looking over the crowd ahead of them, Gaius saw a large man near the edge of the street. Motioning to two of his men to go with him, he called to the stranger, "You there! The tall one. Pick up the cross and carry it to the place of the skull."

The soldiers looked at Gaius in surprise. A Roman soldier could command a citizen to carry his pack for one mile as a part of the obligation as a subject of Rome, but this was stretching that authority a bit. The tall man hesitated a moment, but then saw he had no choice and picked up the cross. Gaius ignored the stares of his men. He would do what he could. It was little enough.

Soon he saw the gate ahead of them. They were almost there. The other group had beaten them to the spot as he thought they would, having prisoners who were in better physical condition for the trip. His eyes surveyed the area for any signs of a band ready to try to break the prisoner free, but there was no such group about. A few women and a man he thought he recognized as one of the followers stood near where the third cross would go, but there was no threat in any of them. The other bystanders appeared to be the usual group of morbid curiosity seekers. There were also, of course, the teacher's enemies, who were there to see that no tricks were pulled, like slipping in a substitute at the last minute.

The fastening of the victim to the cross went swiftly. The men with the hammers and the long spikes worked quickly, and the cross was hoisted into place. People often wondered what actually killed these men, since Rome did not add further torture. Gaius had asked a doctor about it once. Of course, a lot depended on the victims' condition when they got there, but basically, the doctor said, it was death by suffocation and heart failure. The unnatural bending of the arms from the body and the weight of the body hanging as it did crowded the heart and lungs until they could no longer function. It was a slow and agonizing death, and if it were not over by sundown, Roman policy was to break the legs of any victims still alive. The added shock and the further sagging of the body finished the matter quickly. There was one mercy, Gaius thought. This being the day before the Jewish sabbath, the religious leaders would want to finish the crucifixions early so as not to desecrate their holy day. As if the day determined the rightness or wrongness of an act! But now the waiting began.

Gaius had never put in a harder day in his life. The crucifixion itself was no different than scores of others he had seen or been in charge of. He had become somewhat accustomed to them, or more accurately, he had become resigned to them. It went with the job, and for the most part, it seemed to be a worthless lot who died this way . . . thieves, murderers, revolutionaries. He realized with a shock that this was really the only victim he had ever even remotely known. The others had been nameless faces, broken figures on a cross. This one . . . Gaius shuddered to think what he must be. What kind of a man could teach and heal the way he had? What kind of man could have power like that and refrain from using it to his own ends? The wealthy would pay plenty for a private physician such as he was!

The teacher's enemies were taunting him now about coming down from the cross. Gaius saw a few of the less bold ones glance anxiously at the darkening sky. Strange that he hadn't noticed before how dark it was becoming. It was more like an eclipse than heavy clouds, but it was going on too long for that. A bad dust storm from the desert, he supposed. Could it have anything to do with what was happening here?

But only a groan came from the man on the cross, a groan and a cry of thirst. One of the mercy women who brought drugged wine to crucifixions to help dull the pain of the sufferers hurried to him with a sponge on a long stick. Sometimes soldiers tried to keep them back, but Gaius would never let his men do that. Let them offer what they could, he had told the soldiers. But as he watched, he saw the teacher turn his head away. He would not take it. By heaven, there was a man! As if he wanted to know what was going on until the end. Was he expecting something to happen?

Gaius saw a scuffle on the fringe of the crowd and, motioning to his second in command to be alert, he walked over to see what was going on. Was it a belated rescue attempt? He didn't want to order his troops to kill any of this man's friends, and besides, they could not save him now. Between the scourging and the agonizing journey through the streets and the twisted torture already endured, he doubted that the teacher could have made it if they took him down.

The disruption turned out to be only someone who had had his purse snatched. Served him right if he was more interested in what was going on here than in minding his own affairs. Gaius did not hurry back to the crosses. He wished he had asked Pilate to have sent someone else. Maybe Pilate would have understood—whom was he kidding? What kind of army could you have if you started letting soldiers choose their enemies?

Enemy? This man was not his enemy! What was he saying? This wasn't war. It was just some hideous, indiscriminate death, somehow supposed to preserve the empire by striking terror into the hearts of would-be rebels. Peace by terror. It was a strange way. But he confessed to himself that he didn't know a better one. Unless . . . He tore his thoughts away from letting them dwell too long on the way that this man had talked about.

"Love your enemies," Gaius had heard the teacher say that day that seemed so long ago when he had heard him speak. Did the teacher consider him his enemy? he wondered. It seemed a stupid question. Here he was in charge of his crucifixion. Why wouldn't the teacher regard him as an enemy? Or did he recognize the systems and the twisted labyrinth of cirumstances in which people found themselves immersed at times? Was that why he had said what he had when they were fastening him to the cross? "Father, forgive them," the teacher had said. "They know not what they do."

That describes me, all right! Gaius thought. He surely didn't know what he was doing! If only he had a little more time to think! But with whom was the teacher talking when he said that? Suddenly Gaius felt very strange. A funny weakness struck him in the pit of the stomach. Those words had been a prayer. He knew that now. They could be nothing else. And yet they were spoken aloud, so perhaps they had also been intended for him to hear. Had the teacher been praying for him? Asking . . . asking *who* to forgive him? The chill that he had felt a moment before deepened as one answer to that question began to creep into his consciousness.

There was a loud cry from the center cross, and Gaius hurried back. He didn't want to go, but he was a man whom duty had trained very well. Some of the watchers said something about the teacher's calling for Elijah and Gaius wondered who that was, but he quickly forgot it as the figure spoke again. Now that he was closer, he could hear more clearly, and he knew enough of the local language to know that it was not Elijah that the teacher was calling for, but *Eloi*, one of the Hebrew names for their God. It was seldom that a Gentile heard the word at all. The Jews were hesitant to speak the name of their God around Gentiles, and it was said that some would not write the word at all. Gaius had never heard such agony in a voice. It was not a body crying out; it was a spirit. "My God, My God, why have you forsaken me?" There was such passion in the voice that Gaius found himself almost expecting a reply. But he heard nothing. Only silence. Even the murmuring crowd had grown still. They were listening, too. He thought again of his so-close refusal. Maybe it would not have made any difference to the teacher's situation, but it would have made a difference to Gaius!

He looked at the face again, and suddenly he knew that while he had heard nothing and the crowd had heard nothing, that man on the cross had! He saw it in the man's eyes, pain-filled as they were. Gaius did not know what the teacher had heard, and he doubted that he could have understood it if he had, but he was sure that the questioner had been answered. Perhaps the question had not been answered, but the teacher had! Gaius was as sure of that as he was of his own name, and the words that the teacher uttered next confirmed what he had sensed.

"It is finished! Father, into your hands I commit my spirit."

And he was gone. It was not as if he had died so much as a feeling that he was gone. As if he had just . . . left. There was nothing on the cross but an empty shell; before it stood a Roman centurion, fingering the Roman eagle on the handle of his sword and voicing the conviction that would stay with him all his days: "Truly, this was the Son of God!"

9.

TOO GOOD TO BE TRUE

John 20:19-31

Thomas walked alone toward the Essene[1] section of the city of Jerusalem, where ten days earlier he and the other disciples had eaten their final meal with Jesus. It had been a celebration of the Passover. But because the Essenes followed a different calendar than the rest of the Jews, their meal came earlier than the celebrations in the rest of Jerusalem. Where they were to eat had been something of a mystery until Jesus had announced that those who went to make the arrangements were to follow a *man* carrying a water jar. They had guessed easily enough then because the only men in Jerusalem likely to be carrying water were Essene priests. For everyone else, carrying water was regarded as women's work. Besides, the Essenes had a guest house with a triclinium,[2] a room with a three-sided table where they could observe the Passover in the appropriate manner. The disciples' homes would hardly accommodate the twelve.

This was the first time Thomas had been back here since that fateful night, and he did not relish the visit. But he had promised he would come when next they met, and this was the day they had said. He had missed the meeting last week and was shocked and disbelieving when those who were there claimed that Jesus had appeared in their midst. He had heard similar tales from others, too—from the women who went to the tomb the morning after the crucifixion, from the two disciples traveling to Emmaus, and then from the ten. But Thomas simply did not believe that Jesus was alive.

It was not that he didn't want to believe; it wasn't that at all. It was just that . . . well, when you have been knocked down and flattened by life and it seems as if everything you hoped for has fallen apart, good news is received very cautiously. Thomas had made up his mind that he was not going to set himself up for that kind of pain again. Not easily, anyway. So he had listened to the excited testimony of his friends about how Jesus had risen from the grave and had appeared in their midst. But he had shaken his head and said that he would not believe until he saw for himself. Furthermore, he had added, not only did he not trust their eyes, he would not trust his own; he would not believe until he had put his fingers into the wounds to prove that his own eyes were not deceived.

The others had rebuked him then. But they did not seem to understand how much he felt that he had failed Jesus. All of them had, but Thomas felt that he had failed him more than any of the others. Except Judas, of course. After all, when they had tried unsuccessfully to persuade Jesus not to go to Jerusalem for Passover this year, it was he, Thomas, who had declared in foolish bravado, "Then let us go with him that we may die also!" And what had happened? He had fled into the darkness like all the rest of them, afraid for his life.

If that had been all, he might have handled it. But looking

back now, he saw that simply as the culmination of all the misunderstanding and failure he had been a part of while Jesus was alive. Early in Jesus' ministry they had imagined that he was going to set up the promised kingdom right here in Jerusalem. When it finally began to dawn upon them that Jesus was not interested in a political kingdom and the overthrow of Rome, they still expected a kingdom of some kind in which they would share as princes. They had even argued about it along this very street where he walked now, discussing who would sit on his right hand and who on his left. Jesus' rebuke of that attitude had been delivered in a way that was unmistakably a sign that they had misunderstood him again. Letting him wash their feet had been a bit much for them to submit to, but somehow they sensed that if they did not submit to that, something even worse would have happened. They could not imagine what, but they were sure of it nonetheless. So they had sat motionless, wordless, while he circled the table girded with a towel like a common servant. All except Simon. Poor Simon; he could never sit wordless, so he had blurted out, "Lord, you shall never wash my feet!" He had then been reduced to confusion by the quick rebuke that came from Jesus, "Except I wash you, you have no part of me!"

But that had been only the beginning of that evening of failures. There had come that awful moment at the table when Jesus had announced that one of them would betray him. Jesus hadn't said it angrily or accusingly, but it had fallen on that little group like the collapse of a city wall. Why had he not recognized that it was Judas and done something to stop him? It was so clear now whom he had meant. He had said it was one with whom he dipped in the bowl. The way the seating was arranged, that could only have been Judas or

John; and he knew that it couldn't be John. But no, they each had to play the game of asking if he were the one. Of course, they did have ample experience to recognize that they had disappointed him before, but betraying him was much more than that. He could see that now; why couldn't he have seen it then? Even when Judas went out, they only supposed that he was attending to some errand on which the Master had sent him as their treasurer.

Thomas would never forget how Jesus had talked with them after Judas had gone. It was as if he had so much to say and so little time in which to say it. Little had they known how true that was! What he said was beautiful. But while the words burned into their minds, there was much that they did not understand. He told them not to be afraid, to believe in him as they did in God! The Pharisees would have had him for that claim, for sure. He spoke of preparing a place for them, of coming to take them there; he likened himself to a vine and called them the branches; he said that he no longer called them servants, but friends; he prayed a prayer that they would never forget—a prayer for *them* and the struggles that they would have to face, a prayer for unity and courage, a prayer such as they had never heard him pray before. It was almost as if they were not there and he was pouring out his very soul to God in their behalf and of others yet to come—others, who, he said, would come to believe because of them! Even with all of that, he had said there was more that he wanted to tell them but that they were not ready to hear it. Then they had sung one of the Passover hymns, remembering the ancient sacrifice in Egypt when the lambs were killed to mark the houses where the Hebrews lived when the angel of death passed over the land.

Then they had gone out to the garden where he often went when he had some inner struggle to go through. But they had slept while he had struggled! How dense and thoughtless could they be? They had awakened only moments before Judas arrived with the troop of temple guards that led Jesus away. The rest . . . he did not even want to think about the rest of it anymore.

Thomas still was not sure why he had agreed to come to this gathering today. It was painful to come back here to face so many reminders of his shattered dreams and hopes. To have those bitter reminders stirred still more by those who seemed bent on trying to start it all over again was really more than he wanted. But he had made some commitments to these friends, and he would keep his commitments in spite of his doubts.

As he walked the narrow passageways, he thought again of what his friends had told him. What if it were true? He had been thinking of that possibility in spite of his disbelief. Was he disbelieving because he felt the others were overly emotional and had let their feelings and wishes blind them to reality, while he was cool and logical? Did he think that he deserved some special revelation all his own if it were really true, demanding to stick his fingers into the wounds before he would believe? That had bothered him more as he thought about it. Who was he to set up the conditions under which he would believe? It was not his friends from whom he was demanding these conditions. They could do nothing about such things. If there were any reality here, it came from God; so it was from God that he was demanding proof. The thought stopped him in his tracks. Who was he to demand anything from God? A few moments ago he was regarding himself as the greatest of failures; now here he was demanding special revelations!

Thomas walked more slowly now. If this were true . . . But he did not want to let himself think about that. It hurt too much. It implied an opportunity to begin again, as it were; to forget all the old misconceptions and to really listen to what the Master wanted them to do. They had had so many chances to understand that Thomas couldn't conceive of their having another one! But if there were a risen Christ to lead them, there would be no limit to what they could do and where they could go. No journey would be too great for him to make, no risk too much to ask. He would fulfill the rash promise that he had made about being willing to die for Jesus.

Thomas shook his head and quickened his pace. He would not be lured into such painful ways of thinking only to have them dashed in despair again. Far better not to hope too much; then he would not be hurt with disappointment.

He was soon at the gate of the Essene settlement. The latch was open, so he passed inside and climbed the outer stairway to the upper room. He heard the sound of voices before he entered. It sounded as if all of the others were already here. Peter was there, as was Matthew. He could recognize those voices readily enough from among the several that he could hear.

"Welcome, Thomas!" several called at once as he entered the room.

"We were just wondering if you would come," Peter added.

"I said I would be here, didn't I?" Thomas answered with a little warmth.

Andrew smiled his "there-goes-my-brother-talking-too-much-again" smile as he embraced the newcomer without any words. His smile and his embrace said enough, and Thomas felt his resentment at Peter's words fade. Trust Peter to put into words what others might only think! Of course they had wondered about him; he had missed the last gathering, had he not?

Well, he was here now, and seeing these with whom he had shared so much, Thomas knew that he was glad that he had come. The fellowship of these gathered here was enough to warm his heart. And if he could not share their new belief, perhaps he could keep them from acting too foolishly until they had time to ease the anguish that seemed to have gripped their minds and distorted their understandings. Someone had to keep a little calmness and sensible perspective operating in this group. Some had already been talking about proclaiming that Jesus was alive, and that could only bring more trouble. It was not that he feared for his life now. He had gotten beyond that; he would not run again. But if he were to die, let it be for something worthwhile.

It was the expression on Andrew's face that caused him to turn. The heavy door behind him had been shut when he entered, and he had not heard it open. But Andrew was obviously seeing someone behind Thomas. Curious, he turned around. As he turned, he heard a voice that he had been sure he would never hear again, saying, "Peace be with you." It was Jesus.

Thomas stared in disbelief and rubbed his eyes. The figure was still there, and he could not see through him to the wall behind like one might expect of some spirit-figure or apparition. There was real substance there. Even as his mind registered that fact, he saw Jesus hold out his hands and heard him speak his name.

"Thomas, reach your finger here and see my hands, and put your hand in my side and feel my wounds; and be not faithless, but believe."

Jesus stood waiting, his hands extended, but Thomas made no move to approach him. Tears of joy streamed down his face as he fell to his knees and cried, "My Lord and my God!"

NOTES:

1. The Essenes were an important Jewish religious sub-community that flourished during the time of Jesus. Discoveries at Qumran (an Essene settlement) have revealed much more about them than was previously known. Some scholars have suggested that both Jesus and John the Baptist were related to this group. They practiced a communal lifestyle, including the communal ownership of property. One link to their presence in Jerusalem is the record of an "Essene Gate" referred to by Josephus *(Wars of the Jews, 5:142-45)*. Volume 2 of *The Interpreter's Dictionary of the Bible* is a good source for a relatively brief account.

2. A triclinium was a special guest room that featured an open "U" shaped table around which guests reclined for the eating of a meal. The word in the Gospels for "furnished room" (Luke 22:11-12; Mark 14:15) is the word normally used for such a room, and the Gospels clearly speak of this being a reclining meal (John 13:23-25). Remains of tricliniums have been found in Jerusalem from the time of Jesus as well as in Jericho, Neapolis, and other sites. The slide/lecture set by Dr. James Fleming of the Jerusalem Center for Biblical Studies has an excellent treatment of this seating arrangement as it applies to the Last Supper. (Available from Educational Opportunities, Inc., P.O. Box 6067, Lakeland, Florida 33803.)

10.

A DREAM THAT CHANGED HISTORY

Acts 10:1-43

It was a beautiful day in Joppa. The waters of the Mediterranean gleamed like some great jewel in the noonday sun. The cries of sea gulls fighting over scraps of fish carried above the hum of voices on the streets. On the docks the chants of slave crews loading and unloading cargo seemed to belie the harshness of their lives.

On the living area on the top of Simon the tanner's house, a piece of canvas was sailing, repaired and waiting for its owner to claim it. It stirred dreamily in the kind of breeze that had made seashores a favorite place for napping for centuries. In the shade of the sail, a man had been doing just that until a moment ago. Now he was awake.

In spite of his own weariness, the warmth of the sun, the cooling breeze, and the lull of the sound of the sail to blanket the noise of the street, Simon Peter was wide awake. Furthermore, he was drenched with sweat. He had just awakened from a nightmare at noontime.

The nightmare had to do with eating, and no doubt his own

hunger had been a part of its creation. He had been tired and hungry when he came up here to rest. And while the soothing sounds and surroundings had lulled him into sleep, the hunger messages were still being sent to his brain, reinforced no doubt by the odors of the noonday meal being prepared in the house below him. Out of such material, dreams are born.

But it was not a pleasant dream of a fine meal that had awakened him. This dream had caused him great discomfort. He had seen a great sheet descending from heaven. In it were all kinds of animals. Some were a part of any good Jewish diet, and some were those that were forbidden for a Jew to eat or even touch. Their very nearness would have been a source of discomfort because such animals were an abomination and a cause for uncleanness to any devout Jew. As if the proximity of such animals were not enough, Peter had heard a voice saying, "Rise, Peter; kill and eat!" Three times the bidding had come, and three times Peter had turned away in horror. To eat such things was forbidden! Everything in his upbringing told him that. From his mother's knee he had heard the ancient restrictions on the food that made the eater unclean, and the law of his people taught him that uncleanness was an affront to God.

The matter was far more involved than eating meat from an unclean animal. If one of the forbidden insects fell into a container of water, as precious as water was to desert people, the water had to be thrown out and the vessel, if it were of clay, had to be broken and cast away. Furthermore, one had to be careful where one threw the water when emptying the vessel. If the water came in contact with seed for planting, the seed became unclean. If the carcass of an unclean animal so much as touched a stove or an oven, that article had to be broken and discarded. A person who touched such an animal was considered unclean until the sun went down that day. All of this was bad enough. But to eat that which was forbidden, to deliberately and knowingly violate that ancient law, was to risk the wrath of God upon the entire nation. The Book of the Law made cleanness and holiness part and parcel of one another. It was written:

> You shall therefore make a distinction between the clean beast and the unclean, and between the unclean bird and the clean; you shall not make yourselves abominable by beast or by bird or by anything with which the ground teems, which I have set apart for you to hold unclean. You shall be holy to me; for I the Lord am holy.

Men and women had died rather than violate those laws. Every Jewish child was raised with stories of those who had faced death and torture rather than eat pork under the hated conquerors of the past. Even Pilate's legions had balked at killing people who stood submissively before their swords rather than permit the desecration of their holy places.

Perhaps it all seemed foolish to an outsider, but Peter had never thought it so. All his life he had been faithful to the teachings of his faith concerning what he ate. Even in his dream he had blurted out, "No, Lord! I have never eaten anything that is common or unclean."

When you are raised with a constant emphasis on what you do and do not eat, what you do and do not touch, and who you do and do not associate with in order to find favor with God, it is serious business. Call it prejudice if you want, but when it is institutionalized and made a part of your thought system and your way of life for as long as you can remember, you do not change it very easily! Outsiders who criticize and promise drastic changes simply don't realize what is involved. It is not just a matter of doing something a bit differently than before. Behind the doing is the thinking, the understanding, the patterns of behavior that have become instinctive, and yes, the *feeling* that is involved. It isn't as if you were laying aside an old garment for a new one and feeling a little discomfort because you missed the softer folds and the comfortable fit that only wear can bring. It was far more than that. One can stand a little discomfort for what is going to be better eventually. But when you are dealing with a person's feeling for what is right and wrong, you are asking a person, in effect, to become a sinner!

Looking around him, Peter was aware of other sights and sounds and smells that had no doubt pieced together his disturbing dream. Mingled with the odor of food was the smell of the various skins that were curing in the rooms below him. He knew some of them were unclean because a tanner worked with many animals. Even their nearness had bothered Peter when he saw them around him. Then there was the sail; there had been a great rent in it, and someone had evidently brought it to Simon to mend. Peter remembered thinking just before he drifted off to sleep that it seemed like a great sheet stretched above him. His hunger, the awareness of the un-clean animal skins around him, the sail, the voice of his host calling him to come to dinner—all the elements of his dream were there. But the voice that told him to kill and eat—that was another matter. That was not just a dream. He knew that voice far too well to chalk it up to having misunderstood his host's call to dinner for something else. That was the voice that had taught and praised and sometimes rebuked him for too many years for him to be mistaken; it was the voice that had searched out his love that morning by the lake, the voice that bade him come to him on the water, the voice that he had come to listen for in the midst of his confusion and questioning in the months that had passed since the days that he had heard it in the flesh. It was the voice of the Lord. "Rise, Peter; kill and eat."

He was used to that voice telling him unexpected things. It had happened often enough that he could not dismiss it as a dream, no matter how shocking and radical it seemed. The voice's answer to his refusal had struck him deeply. "What God has cleansed, you must not call common." What could it mean? What was the message here for him?

Somehow Peter had the feeling that there was more involved in this experience than some underlying concern over what he might have for lunch in the home of Simon the tanner. He had been with the Christ too long to let it stop with that. For that matter, he could remember Jesus telling the Pharisees on one occasion that it was not what you took into your body that defiled you but the actions that came out of your life. He had passed it off at the time as a part of Jesus' ongoing debate with the Pharisees and never really thought much about it. Now that he considered it, he wondered why he had passed over it so lightly and never pressed Jesus more over what he meant. He supposed it was because he had been living in surroundings that didn't really make an issue of the matter. Most of his friends and acquaintances felt pretty much as he did. And while the matter might enter into a discussion, he was never really put in situations where he would be tested. Now that the followers of Jesus were spreading out from Jerusalem, however, they were going to be in contact more and more with people who had a stronger exposure to non-Jewish ways and who might have strayed more from the traditional Jewish way—like Simon the tanner, for instance. Simon's occupation could hardly be classified as an approved one for a devout Jew, handling the skins of animals that were unclean or that had been killed in ways that rendered them unclean. People brought the skins from all over, and he couldn't possibly know the circumstances around the animals' deaths. He wouldn't even know when he needed to be cleansed.

How did people like Simon manage? he wondered. He had to come in contact with unclean things all the time. For that matter, he had to come in contact with unclean people all the time, too. Peter stopped a moment after that thought. What was he saying? He didn't like the way this thought was leading him, but it was too late to turn back now. Jesus had led him in unexpected places before, and he had never managed to get away when he tried. Anymore, he didn't even want to try. But that didn't mean that sometimes the journeys were not difficult ones.

The thought that had given him pause for a moment concerned another area of uncleanness: the Gentiles. He had heard that some of them were beginning to show interest in the gospel he was proclaiming about Jesus. How should he answer them? Fellowship with the Gentiles had been as forbidden as pork. What would it mean to open the doors of Christian fellowship to include more than the children of the house of Israel? What would his fellow Jews think? What would it mean to his chances of convincing more Jewish people that Jesus was the Messiah? Wouldn't letting the Gentiles in keep his own people out?

It was then that what the voice of Christ had said about the animals in the great sheet came into his mind again. "What God has cleansed you must not call common." What if the vision was really about people instead of food? If Christ could cleanse and forgive him after his denial and cowardice, could He not cleanse a Gentile of whatever sin he might have committed? If one group of people were no less sinners than another, why should one be regarded as more washable?

He smiled at the thought, but it really wasn't a laughing matter. The purity of the race was an issue that ran deep in many cultures. And while he had not given up all of his Jewishness in his allegiance to Christ, he had learned enough from the Master to recognize crumbling walls when he saw them! Peter remembered well how Jesus had not held back from social contact with anyone—Gentiles, Samaritans, tax collectors, harlots, lepers. All those whom so many in his day called unclean Jesus called to himself. He remembered, too, how much opposition that attitude had brought to Jesus.

As he thought about it, Peter realized that he had somehow gone through those days without ever really recognizing that Jesus' example of such openness to all people was to be imitated and not just accepted as something that Jesus did. Now he found himself facing his own long-accepted customs in the light of Jesus' life and a dream on a housetop. Animals and diet were not the issue; people were the issue. For a moment in Peter's mind, the great sheet in his dream held not animals, but people—people of all races and colors and nations. And the sheet became the arms of the Christ, as if Christ were drawing them to himself.

Peter did not know all that would come of this action this day. He had long considered the Gentiles unclean—perhaps not in the same way as unclean animals but not much different either. Since his days with Jesus he had not stressed the matter in the arrogant ways of some that he knew, but still, in the quiet of his own heart he had held on to that separation. It was a "let-them-go-their-way-and-I'll-go-mine" kind of attitude. But he couldn't do that anymore. He had been told to take some initiative, to move forward on his own, to reach out.

What would it mean if he didn't? Would the followers of Jesus be limited only to those who embraced Judaism? Would their number wither and die because their field of harvest was limited? How many who followed Judaism would refuse to believe that Jesus was the Messiah? Would the movement become a little band within the larger Jewish community, like the Essenes? On the other hand, what would happen if the doors of the church were opened to the Gentiles? There were more of them than there are of us, he thought. He shook his head at that same old "we and they" idea. He hadn't intended to look at it that way, but old habits die hard. And that is what much of it was—habit. Like which side of your face you washed first every morning or which sandal you put on first or which side you turned toward when someone called your name from behind. You did those things without thinking, and you always did them the same way. There wasn't a right or wrong to it; it was just the way you had always done it. It was automatic. But when the actions and attitudes that had become automatic involved other people, right and wrong did enter into it.

Peter looked over the edge of the rooftop. Three strangers were approaching the house of Simon the tanner. By the manner of their dress he recognized that they were Gentiles, and somehow he had a feeling they were looking for him.

So soon! Why couldn't they have waited awhile? Could they not have given him time to think about it, to reflect on it, to plan the best way to do it? Why did it have to happen so fast? But then, he thought, quickly or slowly was very much a matter of whether you were the one who was asking for change or the one who was being asked to do the changing. He hardly needed the words of the voice when it came this time. "Rise, and go with them without hesitation for I have sent them." The voice didn't add, "Call nothing common which God has cleansed," but Peter didn't need to hear that said again. He knew that now.

Peter started down the stairway to greet the strangers at the door and to try to follow the dream. Behind him on the rooftop the great canvas sail made another stirring in the wind; a stirring that sounded like the turning of a giant page.

11.

A STREET CALLED STRAIGHT

Acts 9:1-19

Ananias was worried. He was a faithful man and he believed that you should do whatever God tells you to do. But today he was wondering if God ever made mistakes; or at least if you ought not question your hearing now and then.

How did you know when it was God who spoke? Ananias had often secretly wondered if some of the acclaimed messages from God were not echoes of one's own desires and wishes given weight and authority by crediting them to God. He knew that was a terrible thing to say. It impugned people's motives in a manner that was really unjust. Nevertheless, he had seen instances that seemed awfully convenient in their timing. And some of the stories from the early days seemed to reflect a spirit of vengeance and blood that was more in keeping with the mood of those early days than with the kind of compassion and mercy that Jesus of Nazareth, whom he now called Lord, had talked about. Was he to believe that God changed his attitude so greatly? Did it not make more sense to think that it was people who changed and that God's message to them sometimes got a bit molded by the understanding of the times, like water taking the shape of the container you put it in?

Was it wrong to think such thoughts? It was not that he was looking for an excuse to ignore the vision he had had . . . well, at least it wasn't entirely that! He smiled at the realization that he was doing pretty much the very thing that he was wondering about.

He admitted that he would be relieved if he could somehow believe that he didn't have to do what he thought he had to do. More than that, he really wanted to be sure. To risk one's life was bad enough! But to risk it foolishly, wastefully, for nothing . . . well, you could hardly fault someone for not wanting to do that, could you?

But how were you to know!

Ananias soon realized that this line of reasoning was not going to get him out of what he felt he was being asked to do. At least this wasn't coming from his own hidden desires! The last thing in the world that he *wanted* to do was to put himself in the clutches of Saul of Tarsus, to whom he was being sent. Saul was a madman. He had imprisoned Christians all over Jerusalem until the people had scattered like quail in the thickets. Stephen's death had been a great blow to the young church, and while no one claimed that Saul was responsible, he had been there. It was said that he held the cloaks of those who did the stoning. Granted, Stephen had not preached a very tasteful sermon in the circumstances. Calling his hearers "stiffnecked and uncircumcised in heart and ears" and labeling them murders and betrayers because they had killed the Just One who had come into their midst was hardly calculated to win him any friends! And claiming to see God with Jesus standing at his right hand had been the final straw. That was blasphemy of the first order. Given the anger he had already aroused, his death should not have been a surprise. But his loss had been a shock, and this Saul of Tarsus seemed to go berserk shortly afterward. He became like a man obsessed, like a man trying to still a voice inside him by shouting more loudly at those around him.

There had been a few positive results from Saul's persecution, however. Because the homes of Christians were being broken into in Jerusalem and many were being put into prison, Christians were leaving Jerusalem for other places, becoming like the people of Israel in the Great Dispersion. And wherever they went, they carried word of the Christ. It was like scattering a fire; new fires started wherever strong sparks landed.

Now Saul was coming here. The Christian underground had its sources. Word was that Saul had secured papers and authority to arrest and imprison Christians in this city as he had elsewhere, and Ananias had no wish to be one of his early catches. But the voice had been quite clear: "Go to the street called Straight and inquire at the house of Judas the tanner for Saul of Tarsus, for behold, he is praying." But when he expressed his misgivings and reminded God of how much evil this man had already done to the church, he was told to go anyway, that God had a mission for Saul to the Gentiles.

Well, come to think about it, it had been rather silly to try to tell God what Saul had already done. Did he think that God had been out of town or something? Strange how we pray that way sometimes. Praying to the All-knowing by reporting the latest news! But then, it was usually the part of the recent news that most concerned *us,* wasn't it? There was that intrusion of self again.

Maybe, he thought, the answer was that what God really wanted could be tested by measuring it against what he wanted and figuring that if he didn't want it, God did! He had known some who seemed to act that way. Their God was harsh and vindictive, always demanding something more and more difficult. Some people wore hair shirts next to their skin in order to keep themselves uncomfortable. Some tore and mutilated their flesh to prove that their bodies were subject to their spirits. Human nature was regarded as completely depraved and incapable of doing anything good. But if you followed that line of reasoning to its logical conclusion, then abusing the body was equally depraved since it was still a human action. Furthermore, if you assumed that anything God wanted humanity did not, what about the fact that Jesus had taught that God's Spirit would dwell in them? Didn't that mean that we could come to do the right things, some of the time at least? Ananias didn't argue with the fact that one sometimes had to struggle to do what one felt to be right. Just knowing the right was not enough. But it was certainly a good foundation to start with!

But how were you to know?

He knew that he was stalling. There was still the vision he had had, telling him to go to Saul at the home of Judas on the street called Straight.

Ananias sighed and got to his feet. All he could do was go. There was no way he could come up with proof that what he felt he needed to do was the right thing. Searching his heart for poor or twisted motives was all right; in fact, it was essential. But it finally came down to an inner conviction that would not be shaken. He must go to Saul.

He was sure that this was no death wish on his part. He knew full well that martyrdom was the fate of many Christians in his time and might be his, but he was not one of those who believed that dying as a martyr was somehow more important than living faithfully whatever years one was given to live. But if there came a time when one had to risk in order to be faithful, so be it. There were no guarantees of safety; only the promise that the strength would be sufficient. And since he had searched his heart for any clues that this might be some warped direction of his own heart, he could do nothing but act on the basis of what he truly felt this was—a word from God.

What finally convinced him was the inner conviction that he had to follow this voice; a conviction that was so strong he was willing to be judged wrong in order to obey. He was not saying that sincerity was all that mattered. Sincerity was critically important, but one could be sincerely wrong as well as sincerely right. Perhaps even some of our twisted personal motives could be used by God for God's own purposes. After all, if God persisted in using human agents, then much of God's working material was pretty deficient!

Ananias remembered the stories of his boyhood—stories of Abraham and Noah and Joshua and a host of others. They had not been perfect, but they had been faithful. If they had turned aside because the call was too risky or too uncertain, where would he be now? They called Abraham "the father of the faithful" because he went out without knowing where the call would take him. Ananias did not expect such immortality from his obedience, but on the other hand, being remembered as "the father of the careful" was not so terrific a prospect either! He may not be remembered at all for what he was called to do this day. It was this man Saul for whom God seemed to have something in mind. Why should anyone remember Ananias? Who knew the name of the rabbi who had taught the boy Jesus at the synagogue in Nazareth? Did anyone remember him? Did the man himself even know what the fruit of his labors had become?

Well, so be it, he thought. God would remember; that was enough.

The home of Judas on the street called Straight. He didn't know the house, but he knew the street. They called it "Straight" because in a city that was filled with narrow, twisting passageways, this was a street that seemed to defy its environment. One could see its plumbline directness cut among the shops and houses far into the distance. While other walkways branched off at all kinds of angles and curves, this one kept its course.

"It is like God's way!" he said to himself. "Our human journeys twist and turn and wander here and there, but God's way moves with a purpose and a direction that cut across our tangled paths." The thought was like a confirmation of his call.

A short time later Ananias stood in a darkened room and prayed with a man who, for three days, had been blind. Ananias called Saul "brother." Something like scales fell from Saul's eyes, and the Holy Spirit came upon him. Ananias knew then that he had chosen the right way. But like many a man or woman who followed that Voice, the knowing came only in the obedience of walking a street called Straight, wherever that journey led.

QUESTIONS FOR REFLECTION

QUESTIONS FOR REVIEW.

"Redigging Old Wells"

————————

1. How does envy cause problems in our world today?

2. Is it more difficult to accept the success of a neighbor or a close friend than of some unknown person you may read about in the paper? Why?

3. When we admire the courage of our ancestors, what consideration do we give to the faith and beliefs that gave them their courage?

4. What instances can you think of in which justice has been denied to the wealthy?

5. What are examples of "old wells" that you have visited with joy?

"Water from Bethlehem"

———————————

1. Can you think of any place or experience that compares to David's memories of Bethlehem? What are they?

2. What do the actions of David's men tell you about their feeling for him?

3. What do David's actions with the water tell you about his feeling for his men?

4. Does "water from home" really taste better than any other? Why?

5. How do we offer to God the gifts that come to us from others?

"The Third Day"

1. What attitudes and opinions do you think Mary might have had to endure after it was learned that she was pregnant before her marriage to Joseph?

2. What kind of man do you think Joseph must have been to have accepted Mary's story of what had happened?

3. Why do you think God chose a humble maiden to bear the Christ instead of an older, devout woman such as the mother of John the Baptist?

4. Does "Mary's song" tell you anything about her expectations concerning the expected Messiah? Did Jesus' ministry fit the image that Mary seemed to expect? How?

5. Do you think that Mary's expectations of what her son would someday be influenced the way she brought up her child? Is there a difference between raising a child for a great and noble cause and imposing our own expectations upon our children? How do we walk that line?

"A View from the Ditch"

──────────

1. Why do you think the priest or the Levite might have passed by without helping the injured man?

2. Do you think most people would stop to help someone who was injured in a situation such as the one in the story? Why?

3. Have you ever passed up an opportunity to help someone who appeared to need help? If so, how did you feel about it afterwards?

4. Do you think our society's quickness to sue for damages stifles the "good Samaritan" impulse? What is the alternative?

5. Does the fact that someone may have gotten into trouble because of their own bad decision change our obligation to help? Why or why not?

"Opinion Poll in Caesarea"

_____

1. Consider paragraphs one and two. How would you summarize Jesus' problem with the twelve? Does every conscientious teacher ask himself or herself this sort of question?

2. With regard to spiritual things and the understanding of the kingdom of God, is a high I.Q. or other intellectual prowess any advantage to a learner? Why or why not?

3. Is it conceivable that the twelve could have utterly failed to understand Jesus' message? If so, what alternatives could Jesus have taken?

4. Is Jesus' first question, "Who do men say that the Son of man is?" still relevant today? If yes, how?

5. Is an answer to Jesus' second question, "Who do you say that I am?" required of everyone who would profess faith in Christ today? Why?

6. Why were these questions, especially the second, so crucial to Jesus' mission?

7. Why do you think that Jesus charged the twelve to tell no one that he was the Christ?

8. How do you understand Peter's role as the "rock" upon which the Christian church is built? In what sense is Peter given the keys of the kingdom?

"Nightfall"

—————————

1. How could one who had been so intimately exposed to Jesus betray him?

2. Why did Judas betray Jesus?

3. Why had Judas followed Jesus? What had he expected Jesus to do?

4. How did Judas visualize Christ's kingdom? Why was Jesus not able to convince him that his kingdom was different than the image Judas held?

5. Can you think of any ways today in which we seek to force Christ into molds of our own making? Do we ever betray him when he does not respond as we think he should? Give some examples.

"Verdicts from Strangers"

---

1. Why do you think Jesus would not let himself be used by the revolutionaries?

2. Jesus seemed much in sympathy with the common people and their plight. Why do you think he did not urge them to overthrow their oppressors?

3. If John's chronology of events is correct, what symbolism do you see in the fact that Christ died as the lambs for the Passover were being offered?

4. What part of the crucifixion narrative speaks to you most as evidence of the humanity of Christ? Of his divinity?

5. Which of the two thieves do you feel expressed the more typical attitude in the face of death?

"A Centurion's Conviction"

_____

1. Does concern for our future make us fearful of refusing a distasteful task?

2. How do we weigh our moral values when our position is threatened?

3. Was Flavius making a faith statement or simply reflecting his understanding of authority in his response to Jesus' offer to heal his servant?

4. To what extent did any of the chief participants of this event, Jesus, Pilate, or Gaius, have a real choice?

5. What evidence moved Gaius to say that Jesus was the Son of God?

"Too Good to Be True"

———————————

1. Do you think Thomas was justified in questioning the report of the other disciples concerning the resurrection of Jesus? Why or why not?

2. Must we always accept the reports of the experiences of other Christians as valid? Why?

3. Is doubt always a negative emotion? Can you think of events or situations that have been improved or bettered because someone questioned the answers or assumptions of others? Give some examples.

4. Do you think Thomas's doubts may have been rooted in his own emotions and experiences more than in the events themselves? What about the doubts that people have today?

5. What can we do today to help people who doubt find the kind of fellowship in which their doubts might be dealt with?

"A Dream That Changed History"

----

1. How do we hear Christ's message of love in the midst of our own traditions and customs?

2. Who or what do modern-day Christians regard unclean that might compare with the Jewish ideas in which Peter had been brought up?

3. Where are we most challenged today by the call to inclusiveness?

4. What are some of the ways in which we recognize God speaking to us today?

5. How important are rules and disciplines in maintaining any religious faith? How do we decide if and when they should be changed?

"A Street Called Straight"

_____

1. Is it all right to question something that we think God wants us to do? How can we always be sure that a call is from God and not some twisting of our own wishes?

2. What might be some tests that we could apply to urgings that we feel come from God?

3. How do you think you would have felt if you had been told to go to Paul as Ananias was, given what he knew about Paul's activities? Do you think you would have gone?

4. Do you think the feeling that they needed to follow some particular course of action always came to people in Bible days as some overpowering, irresistible order from God? How do we hear the word of God to us for our time?

5. Can you think of any experience in which you felt you should do something you did not want to do? Did you do it? What was the result?

Bell - telephone
only

Carl E. Price is Senior Minister at First United Methodist Church in Midland, Michigan. During his career he has served a wide range of churches, from an eight-point rural curcuit to the inner city.

Dr. Price, a nature enthusiast, has directed trail camps in Michigan and New Jersey. He enjoys many outdoor activities, including hiking, camping, and nature photography.

Other books by the author include *Writings in the Dust* and *Worship without Walls* for The Upper Room and *Trails and Turnpikes*.